The Songwriter's Guide to Protecting Your Songs and Collecting Your Money (U.S. Version)

Bill O'Hanlon, Nancy Deckant, Leslie Bowe

Published by DBO Press

Table of Contents

Acknowledgments

We offer our deepest appreciation to our circle of friends, co-writers and esteemed industry professionals who have helped shape this book. Your generosity and expertise left an indelible mark on our lives and we are truly grateful.

Thank you Lucy LeBlanc, Michelle Canning, Donna Britton Bukevicz, Chris Ising, Ashley Alfermann, George Salamacha, Chuck Allen Floyd, Christopher Hugan, Bob Dellaposta, Shar'n Clark, Debbie Zavitson, Barry Shrum and Zach Green.

A very special shout out to Shar'n Clark whose 30 years of publishing administration experience saved us from crashing on the rocks…more than once!

Appreciation to Nancy Deckant for the cover design that captured the essence of our vision.

Back Cover Photograph Credit: Tori Perry Photography

Introduction

Who Are We and Why This Book?

We are three songwriters who have been writing songs for years and have written thousands of songs between us.

When we first got serious about becoming professional songwriters, we were clueless about the business side of songwriting. We had so many questions!!!

How do we get paid?

Are we supposed to copyright every song we write?

Will someone steal our songs and make money from them and if so, how can we stop them from doing that?

It literally took years to learn about the income and legal side of this creative endeavor of songwriting, because none of the answers are in one place and some were confusing or overwhelming.

One day we met at one of our favorite Nashville meet-ups, Zach Green's "Red Door Hang" and started talking about how we wished there was a straightforward guide to the business side of songwriting.

Bill has authored forty books before. Nancy is a songwriter, song plugger, and publisher. Les previously gathered a significant amount of research for an informational book he wrote for songwriters.

Given our experience, we decided to collaborate on crafting the book we yearned for when we first embarked on our journeys to become professional songwriters.

As friends, colleagues, and co-writers, we joined forces, combining our resources to create the book we longed for during those early days of pursuing our careers as songwriters.

Since we live in the United States (U.S.) we'll cover the essentials needed for songwriters in our country. If you live in another country, note that the details may vary significantly. Seek guidance from organizations in your country.

We Are Self-Administered Songwriters!

We wrote this book for **self-administered songwriters**, individuals managing their own publishing, rather than those signed to a publisher.

Understand we are giving you our hard-won knowledge and experience from the business we love. None of us are attorneys and things in the songwriting and the music business can and do change over time.

You *must* verify what we have told you. Most importantly before taking any major steps like signing any contract, we advise consulting an entertainment lawyer.

From Passion to Profession: Monetizing Your Music

If you're aiming to turn your passion into a profession, you need to know how to generate income from your music, protect your songs from copyright infringement, and make sure you get the proper credit.

This book is about the essential steps that need to be taken to manage the songwriting business and having it all into one place!

Additionally, the music business has changed so much over the recent years with the introduction of new forms of royalties that everyone needs to know about.

We'll give you a step-by-step guide with checklists and links to resources to help make sure you are legally protected and earning all the money due to you from your music.

The Essentials

Remember, this is a guide not the bible! We're keeping it to about 100 pages of the everyday important know how!

- Thirteen royalties that generate income for you.

- New royalties from The MLC, direct licensing and social media.

- Guidelines for copyrighting your song (and when not to bother).

- How to release your own song.

- Step-by-step guide for issuing mechanical licenses.

- Understanding sync licensing and metadata.

Avoiding Distractions: Steering Clear of Major Label Terrain

Last, because our mission is to help independent songwriters, this book ***will not*** delve extensively into areas associated with major label artists, as these are seldom significant sources of income unless a songwriter deliberately directs their attention towards them. These topics include:

- International royalty collection.

- Royalties from derivatives: medleys, mash-ups, parodies, remixes, samples of your song in other artist's work, etc.

- Royalties from ringtones, karaoke tracks and greeting cards.

We hope this book helps you as much as it helped us to write it.

Links to websites and tutorials can and do expire. Visit our website for updates. https://www.nashvillecool.com/tsg

1. The Big Overview

The music business is a big puzzle where copyright rules and business savvy are the secret sauce to self-administered songwriters' cash flow. As a **"rights holder"** in this context, it's crucial to understand the sources of your royalties and the necessary steps for collection.

There's lots to unpack! But don't worry we're going to demystify this for you!

Reminder: Every country has its own royalty collection societies; our focus is on the way it works in the U.S.

Splitting the Copyright Pie

Every song released to the public for sale is made up of the composition and the recording.

The Composition, legally protected by the © copyright, is divided into two parts:

> **The "Writer Share"** (50%) is the creative part of the song, the lyrics and melody.

> **The "Publisher Share"** (50%) is the business side of the song. As a self-administered songwriter, you are the publisher responsible for finding ways to monetize your song, register it with royalty collection organizations and issuing licenses.

The Recording (aka Master or Master Recording), legally protected by the ℗ Phonogram, is what is released to the public for sale. If you pay a producer to make the tracks, sing it or pay for someone to do the vocals, you own the master. If another artist wants to record your song, they can license the composition from you and record their own master. If they pay for the recording, they own it!

Both the composition and recording can generate income through royalties and licensing agreements.

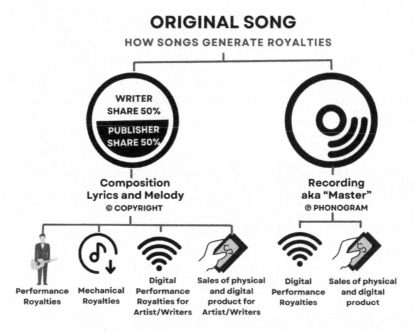

ORIGINAL SONG
HOW SONGS GENERATE ROYALTIES

WRITER SHARE 50%

PUBLISHER SHARE 50%

Composition
Lyrics and Melody
© COPYRIGHT

Recording
aka "Master"
℗ PHONOGRAM

Performance Royalties

Mechanical Royalties

Digital Performance Royalties for Artist/Writers

Sales of physical and digital product for Artist/Writers

Digital Performance Royalties

Sales of physical and digital product

COPYRIGHT © 2024 WWW.NASHVILLECOOL/PRESS

How Songs Generate Royalties in the U.S.

Many aspiring songwriters start their journey by releasing their own music. If this is your situation, start by focusing on the first four royalties listed below.

Should your music catch fire with other artists who want to record your songs, or you decide to get sync placements in TV and film; then you truly need to start moonlighting as your own publisher!

As you learn how royalty's work and do the footwork needed to collect them, the business may become overwhelming. But realize you're not alone. Hey, we were overwhelmed writing this book! But we're trying to keep it simple.

The following is an overview of **what** royalties you can collect. In subsequent chapters, we'll roll up our sleeves and dive deep into the nitty-gritty details of **how** to collect these royalties. Be sure to check out the chart below for a summary of royalties, their purposes, and the organizations tasked with their collection.

1) **Performance Royalties** are generated by the composition both in the U.S. and internationally and are paid to self-administered songwriters when the song is streamed or performed live—either by you or someone else—or played in a venue as recorded music.

   These 'performances' occur anywhere your song is played including terrestrial radio, television, bars, restaurants, concerts, Muzak, overhead music, books, jukebox, karaoke machines, Shazam, etc. These royalties flow to you through your Performance Rights Organization (PRO).

2) **Mechanical Royalties** are generated whenever a composition is reproduced as CDs, vinyl, digital downloads and streams. You'll receive royalties by issuing a mechanical license to the recording owner (artist, label, etc.) and also by registering your song with The Mechanical Licensing Collective (The MLC).

3) **Master Royalties** are generated by the sales of products such as CDs, vinyl, digital downloads and also streams from digital service providers (DSPs). Recording owners collect these royalties directly from the music distributors such as DistroKid, TuneCore and CDBaby, etc.

4) **Digital Performance Royalties** are generated by the composition and the recording for non-interactive streaming on platforms like Internet radio, Pandora, Cable/Satellite radio. These digital performance royalties are paid to the recording owner, artist and non-featured performers by SoundExchange; and if the artist happens to be the writer on the song, a performance royalty is also sent to the PRO.

5) **Royalties from Internet Usage** are generated by the composition when your music is used in posts, reels and videos on platforms like Instagram, TikTok, YouTube. These royalties flow through your PRO.

6) **Direct Licensing Agreements** bypass the PRO and arise from various scenarios. Companies access commercially released

music (not necessarily your songs) and use it as part of their product such as Peloton, Snapchat, X, etc. The NMPA.org and Music Reports negotiate licenses with these companies then collect and distribute royalties to members of their organizations. Another avenue for directly licensing music to retail venues is through overhead radio. Every time you hear music at Target, it could be your song, as they use overhead radio for their playlists.

7) **Black Box Royalties** are generated by the composition when incorrect numbers were assigned and the rights holder could not be found. These royalties will flow from The MLC.

8) **Print Royalties** are generated by the composition for use of lyrics on MusicNotes, LyricFind or wherever you find lyrics.

9) **Synchronization (Sync) Licensing Royalties** are generated by the composition when your song is used in audio-visual media like movies, TV shows, commercials, games, etc. Upfront payments are made when sync licenses are issued by the licensing companies like production companies, music libraries, music supervisors and sync agents.

10) **Master Use Royalties (Sync)** are generated by the recording when it is used in audio-visual media like movies, TV shows, commercials, games, etc. Upfront payments are made when sync licenses are issued by the licensing companies like music supervisors, sync agents, production libraries, etc.

11) **Sync-Related Back End Royalties** flow through your PRO every time a TV, game, etc. with your composition in it is aired, everywhere except for movies in theaters in the U.S.

12) **Sync Licenses for YouTube Videos:** Income is generated through the direct licensing of your composition for inclusion in artists' YouTube videos.

13) **Neighboring Rights Royalties** are generated by the composition and recording in foreign countries when your song is played on terrestrial radio, TV, and in bars. International performance royalties for the composition flow to you through your PRO. You'll need a publishing administrator to collect royalties for your recording and mechanical licenses. Much more to come on this later.

Chapter 1 charts at https://www.nashvillecool.com/tsg

Summary of Music Royalties

Royalty	Description	Composition	Recording
Performance Royalties	U.S. Plays: AM/FM radio, bars, back-end sync, interactive and non-interactive (Note 1)	ASCAP, BMI, SESAC, GMR	N/A
Performance Royalties	International Plays Same places as above (Note 1)	ASCAP, BMI, SESAC, GMR	N/A
Mechanical Royalties	Reproductions of physical products and digital downloads	Songwriter issues mechanical license to recording owner	N/A
Mechanical Royalties	U.S. streaming and some downloads from DSP's	The MLC	N/A
Mechanical Royalties	International streaming and downloads; U.S. "pass-through downloads" (Apple, Amazon)	Music distributor pays to recording owner (See Note 2)	N/A
Master Royalties	Sales of physical products like CDs, vinyl, and digital downloads	N/A	Music distributor sends sales revenue to recording owner (Note 2)
Master Royalties		N/A	Direct sale to fan
Digital Performance Royalties	Non-interactive streaming for internet radio, Pandora, SXM, cable music	ASCAP, BMI, SESAC, GMR (if artist/writer)	SoundExchange
Internet Usage Micro-Content	Songs used in posts and videos on TikTok, FB, Instagram, YouTube	ASCAP, BMI, SESAC, GMR	N/A
Direct Licensing	Negotiated agreements with companies using music like Peloton, X, Snapchat, etc.	NMPA, Music Reports, Overhead Radio	N/A
Black Box Royalties	Unmatched royalties from DSPs, music stores, etc.	The MLC	N/A
Print Royalties	Reproductions of sheet music and lyrics	MusicNotes, LyricFind (also via Distrokid)	N/A
"Sync" Royalties	Upfront royalties for song licensed to movies, TV shows, commercials, video games	Direct license for use of composition	Direct license for use of recording
"Sync" Royalties	"Back end" royalties for airing of your song in movies, TV, commercials, games, etc.	PRO: ASCAP, BMI, SESAC, GMR	N/A
"Sync" Royalties	Song used in video on YouTube. royalty based on ad revenue	Direct license with recording owner	N/A

Note 1: Royalties paid on any commercially released music including Muzak, books, jukebox, karaoke machines, etc.
Note 2: The songwriter & publisher mechanical royalties are included in sales revenue sent to recording owner.

2. Performance Royalties Explained

What are performance royalties and how do you get them?

Performance royalties are payments that songwriters
and publishers receive when their songs are performed or played in
public.

These royalties are compensation for use of your compositions
which are collected and distributed by performing rights
organizations (PROs). In the U.S. that's BMI, ASCAP, SESAC
GMR, and more.

PROs in the U.S. maintain reciprocal agreements with international
PROs. Consequently, both U.S. and international royalties, also
referred to as neighboring rights, flow to you through your PRO.
There is no need for a publishing administrator to handle the
collection of performance royalties for your composition.

How Performance Royalties Are Generated in the U.S.

Here are four key performance royalties that flow through PROs:

Broadcast Royalties: Earned when a song is played on
terrestrial radio (FM/AM), bars, clubs or cable/satellite radio,
Muzak, overhead music, books, jukeboxes, karaoke machines,
greeting cards, social media apps, etc.

Digital Performance Royalties are generated by interactive
streaming platforms like Spotify, Apple Music, Amazon, etc.
as well as non-interactive streaming on internet radio,
cable/satellite radio, Pandora.

Sync-Related Back-End Royalties are generated every time a TV, game, etc. with your composition is aired. Royalties from movies are collected when the film is aired on television and streaming services. (Royalties are not paid on songs aired in movies in theaters.)

Live Performance Royalties are generated when a song is performed live in public venues like concerts, clubs, or festivals by you or someone else.

The following flowchart illustrates most royalties generated by compositions through your PRO.

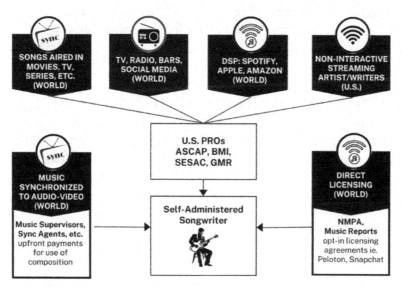

COMPOSITION
HOW ROYALTIES FLOW FROM PLAY TO POCKETBOOK

To collect performance royalties, here's what you need to do.

1) Choose a PRO.

2) Sign up with a PRO.

3) Register your songs.

4) Register songs played live in venues with a PRO license.

Choose a PRO

In the U.S. the performing rights organizations open to all songwriters are BMI and ASCAP. SESAC and GMR are by invitation only.

PROs offer an array of resources, workshops, and networking events. To make the right choice for you, consider your professional goals and which organization aligns best with your needs.

We have often been told, "Reach out to your PRO, they'll recommend you to publishers!" We do believe that it's true for some people, but these days, there are so many songwriters seeking assistance, it can be tough to even get a meeting with a member rep at a PRO, no less a referral. So don't feel bad if you can't get through…and try anyway. It might just happen for you!

By all means, if a PRO representative takes an interest in your career and offers support, that's a good sign to go with that PRO.

Which PRO pays more for a hit song? We have thoughts on this but things change so often depending on the calculations each organization uses it could be misleading to say. Let's go with - they're comparable. When you get a hit song, compare your income with your co-writers in another collection society and you'll know for sure.

But wait, there's more to consider regarding which PRO to join!

The Publishing Company Option

As soon as you select a PRO, you need to decide whether you want to create a publishing company, or not.

Publishing companies with PROs, are not the same as having an incorporated legal company that pays taxes. It means that the rights to your songs are managed by that publishing entity. If someone wants to license a song, your publishing company is where that license will come from.

We recommend setting up a publishing company with your PRO. It simplifies song ownership and song splits and gives you a more professional image. And in some cases, it can be downright detrimental if you *don't* have a publishing company with a PRO.

BMI versus ASCAP: Digging into the details

ASCAP: If you are with ASCAP, you absolutely *__must have__* a publishing company. If you are only registered with ASCAP as a writer, you'll only receive your **writer's share** of performance royalties. Halfsies! Noooo! We all want wholesies right??? Sign up as a publisher on ASCAP.

BMI: BMI is a whole different story. Currently it's $150-250 to set up a publishing company. Whew, that's a budget-buster! But unlike ASCAP, if you don't have a publishing company, the **publisher share** can be added to your writer share. There is no immediate pressure to set up a publishing company.

Oh music business, how you like to keep us guessing!!!

Joining a PRO: What You'll Need

Songwriters often ask, do I need to sign up to more than one PRO? The answer is: Nope! You only need to sign up with **one** PRO.

The specific steps and information needed to sign up varies between PROs and regions. We're going to hit the highlights.

This is how the process generally goes:

1) **Create an Account Online**: Go to the PRO's website and look for the "Creator" option. Enter your personal and contact information, including your legal name, address, phone number, email address, banking information.

2) **Enter Publishing Company Info:** When designating a publishing company, your company's EIN number is needed for incorporated companies. If you don't have an incorporated company, your Social Security Number can be used instead.

3) **Alternative Names:** Be prepared to submit several alternative publishing company names to find a name that isn't taken already. If you have an incorporated publishing company; your PRO publishing company name doesn't have to be exactly the same.

   Choose a catchy name that suits your personality! Take, for instance, Chris Wallin, the renowned songwriter behind Kenny Chesney's smash hit "Don't Blink." He christened his publishing company as "You Passed On My Publishing." Those of us who've been overlooked by big-time publishers can appreciate this snarky-good moniker.

4) **Wait for Approval:** The PRO will review your application and once approved, you'll receive a confirmation of your membership.

5) **Save Your Membership Number:** Once approved your PRO will then assign you a member number which is only important when talking with the PRO. This is **not** the most important number.

6) **Save your IPI/CAE Number:** Once you are in the PRO's system, they will email you separate writer and publishing IPI/CAE numbers. These numbers go on every song that you write. Keep them readily available. You'll need to give them to your co-writers. If your songs get registered under a wrong number, the money your song makes will go to some other song or the black box! We'll cover this later!

Song Ownership: Calculating Song Splits

Song ownership is straightforward when you write it all by your lonesome. It's a 50/50 split that looks like this:

Your writer share is 50%
Your publisher share is 50%

By copyright law, when you co-write with others, you and your co-writer(s) split the composition ownership equally:

For two writers the percentages look like this:
Writer share: You 25%, Your cowriter 25%
Publisher share: You 25%, Your cowriter 25%

Even-steven is how we usually split the composition in Nashville. But in NY and LA the split is usually NOT even and depends more on who contributed what to the song.

Last, break out the calculator if your co-writer happens to have a "co-publishing" deal, where their publisher share is divided between two different publishers. Let's savor some pie charts!

CALCULATING SONG SPLITS

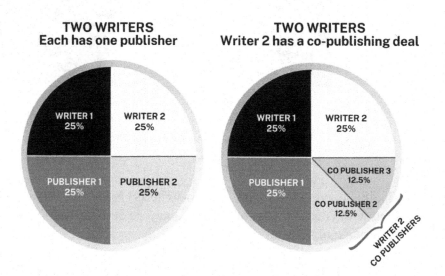

TWO WRITERS
Each has one publisher

WRITER 1 25%   WRITER 2 25%
PUBLISHER 1 25%   PUBLISHER 2 25%

TWO WRITERS
Writer 2 has a co-publishing deal

WRITER 1 25%   WRITER 2 25%
PUBLISHER 1 25%   CO PUBLISHER 3 12.5%
CO PUBLISHER 2 12.5%
WRITER 2 CO PUBLISHERS

Just when you thought you had calculating song splits all figured out, here comes the music business, adding a dash of chaos to keep you on your toes!

If your PRO is ASCAP or SESAC, you are good to go calculating song splits as we've discussed. Your song should add up to 100% no matter how many writers and publishers there are.

But BMI calculates song splits differently. The writer share adds up to 100% and the publisher share adds up to 100% making the total worth of the song 200%.

Let's embark on the pie chart adventure once more, just to make sure you're not accidentally visualizing a pizza!

CALCULATING SONG SPLITS

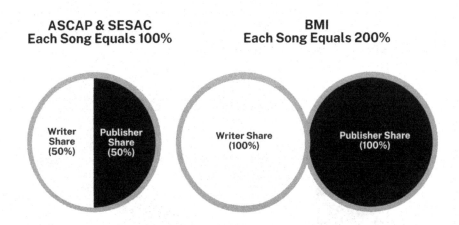

ASCAP & SESAC
Each Song Equals 100%

Writer Share (50%) | Publisher Share (50%)

BMI
Each Song Equals 200%

Writer Share (100%) | Publisher Share (100%)

Finally, always check with your co-writer(s) *before* registering a song with your PRO to make sure you agree on who owns what percentage of the song.

The best thing you can do when you're writing a song with others is to document your percentages on a song split sheet. This handy document will ensure that your co-writers have a crystal-clear understanding of the ownership of the song and access to all the essential PRO information. Go to Chapter 11 has a sample Song Split Sheet.

Ready, Set, Register Your Songs

In this section, we'll cover the essential elements of song registration with your PRO. You don't need to worry if you haven't recorded the song yet; a recording is not required.

We recommend registering all your songs as they are written because, with time, it's easy to forget important details. Here's a list of information you'll need.

Must-Have Information

1) Song title

2) All writer(s) legal name, IPI/CAE, and song split percentage

3) All publisher(s)' PRO Company Name, IPI/CAE, and song split percentage

4) Original Song or Public Domain (PD): Indicate whether the song is original or in the public domain. PD songs are any composition written before 1923. Since you just wrote the song, it's not in the public domain.

5) Samples: Specify if the song contains any samples (Y/N). Samples are pieces of another writer's composition or recording in your song, like if you want to add the chorus of Billie Eilish's "Bad Guy" into your newly written song. Avoid using samples in your recordings; it can be challenging and expensive to get permission to use them in your song.

Other Important Information

6) Song Duration: If the song isn't recorded yet, you can enter an estimated duration of 3 minutes. The PRO is primarily interested in songs with durations over 5 minutes because those songs fall into a different payment category.

7) Song Release Details: Include song release details such as the release date, recording artist(s), album name, and record label if you have this information. If the song hasn't been released yet, you can revise these details in the future.

Once your song is registered, the PRO will assign an International Standard Musical Work Code (ISWC), a unique identifier for your composition. Each song only has *one* ISWC.

This ISWC is crucial for tracking the use of your song worldwide. People who license your songs; like record labels, sync agents and publishers, will ask for the ISWC.

Getting Paid for Your Live Music Performance Earnings

Live Play: If you or *anyone* for that matter, plays your original song at bars, restaurants or any live venue that hold music licenses from your PRO, you can claim those live performances through your PRO and earn money.

> Bill hadn't bothered to officially log his live performances when he played his original songs at songwriter rounds in Nashville. It wasn't until he heard a fellow songwriter mention, "It's really worth it. I cover a significant chunk of my monthly rent by reporting my performances through BMI Live."

> In another situation altogether, Bill has a friend who collaborated on a song with the lead singer of a touring band signed to a major label. During their recent tour, this band performed their song at every concert. Bill's friend obtained the setlist from a tour crew member and reported those live concert performances in the ASCAP ONSTAGE section of his ASCAP account, resulting in additional income.

To receive live performance royalties, navigate to your PRO's live performance portal: BMI Live, ASCAP OnStage, or SESAC Live Performance. Enter the details:

- List the songs that you performed at the gig (songs must be registered with the PRO already).
- The date played.
- Select the venue where you played from the list.

If the venue holds a license with your PRO, you can expect to see it listed. If the venue doesn't have a license it won't appear on the list. If you add the venue to your PRO's database, the venue is likely to be contacted and required to obtain a blanket license for use of music.

> Enter a venue on this list at your own risk. Nancy once had a wake-up call when a disgruntled bar owner was contacted by her PRO to purchase a license for his bar after she entered his bar into the list. Let's just say he was not happy.

Monitor Your Royalties

Last, once your songs are registered and start earning money, your PRO will issue a quarterly report of royalties which can be accessed through their online portal.

Make sure the songs released to the public are receiving royalties. Royalties generally take 6 months to a year or more to land in your account. So be patient!

Look at the different types of usage: what's happening on social media? What's happening internationally? These are powerful signs that your music is breaking through. Look for missing songs and errors.

> We have two songwriter friends who have similar names. Sometimes the more famous writer gets the other songwriter's royalties. This is why it is important to get a song split sheet filled out with the relevant IPI/CAEs rather than just relying on someone's name when you register your songs.

Checklist for PRO Sign-Up

1) **Choose A PRO:** Start by identifying the performing rights organizations that represent songwriters in your region or country. In the United States, most aspiring songwriters opt for ASCAP or BMI.

   a) **ASCAP Membership:** Currently, ASCAP membership costs $50 for writers and an additional $50 for publishers.

   b) **BMI Membership:** BMI offers free membership for songwriters, while publisher membership comes at a fee of $150 for a sole proprietorship and $250 for a corporation.

c) **SESAC Membership:** SESAC's focus is artists and is by invitation only.

d) **GMR Membership:** Top performing songwriters by invitation only.

2) **Decide if registering a publishing company** with your PRO is right for you.

a) **ASCAP: Register a Publishing Company**: If you're with ASCAP, you *must* register a publishing company to get not only your writer's share of the royalties, but also the publisher share.

b) **BMI: Consider Your Options:** It's pricey. your publisher share can be added to your writer share. No rush.

3) **Sign Up with A PRO:** Sign up online with your chosen PRO.

a) ASCAP https://www.ascap.com

b) BMI https://www.bmi.com

c) SESAC https://sesac.com

d) GMR https://globalmusicrights.com

4) **Save Your Writer and Publisher IPI/CAE Numbers:** Your PRO will send these to you by email.

Checklist for PRO Song Registration and Live Show

1) **Collect Co-Writers' PRO Info:** Before registering, gather your song split details and co-writers' PRO information. Register the song promptly after writing it.

2) **Register Your Song with Your PRO:** Go to your PRO's website and register your song. You don't need a recording, just the title, writer(s) legal names, writer IPI/CAE number, publisher(s) company name and IPI/CAE number, and optionally, the song's duration.

    a) Go to our website for **How-To-Videos** for ASCAP and BMI Song Registration.

3) **Live Performances:** Add your set list for all songs you've written that are performed live to your PROs live performance section. Select the date and venue. Again, it doesn't matter if you or someone else performed the song.

4) **Monitor Your Income Statements:** Look at the different types of usage: what's happening on social media? What's happening internationally? These are powerful signs that your music is breaking through. Look for missing songs and errors.

Chapter 2 charts at https://www.nashvillecool.com/tsg

3. Mechanical Royalty Essentials

Mechanical Royalties are generated whenever a composition is reproduced as CDs, vinyl, digital downloads and streams.

How Mechanical Royalties Are Generated in the U.S.

There are two different ways that self-administered songwriters receive mechanical royalties:

You Issue a Mechanical License for a Commercial Release of Your Song: A recording owner, usually an artist or label; comes to you directly wanting permission to record and release a song that you wrote. The recording owner can be a stranger or a co-writer. You will issue a mechanical license and depending on the circumstance, they will pay you upfront or you'll receive quarterly payments. (More to come on this.)

Digital Distribution: The recording owner who licensed the song from you, then releases the song to the public through a digital music distributor. Some royalties from digital downloads and streams flow to you through The Mechanical Licensing Collective (The MLC). Others flow to the recording owner through their music distributor.

Because the music business seems to be on a secret mission to make our lives as tangled as a pair of earphones at the bottom of a backpack, we'll need to dig deeper!

Let's start by looking at what The MLC is collecting and disbursing to songwriters and publishers.

Royalties for Interactive Streaming

Whenever a song is interactively streamed _inside_ the U.S. through a DSP, a mechanical royalty is sent to The Mechanical Licensing Collective (MLC) who disperses the royalty to the self-administered songwriter. Easy peasy!

Whenever a song is interactively streamed _outside_ the U.S., from a foreign country, the DSP sends the royalty to the recording owner through their music distributor.

Royalties for Digital Downloads

When a download is purchased _inside_ the U.S. a mechanical royalty is sent to The MLC unless the DSP opts to have the royalty "pass through" to the recording owner through the music distributor. Apple and Amazon, the most frequent sellers of downloads, are "pass through downloads". The MLC does not collect these royalties!!!

Whenever a download is purchased _outside_ the U.S. from foreign countries, The MLC "pass through downloads" go directly to the recording owner via the music distributor.

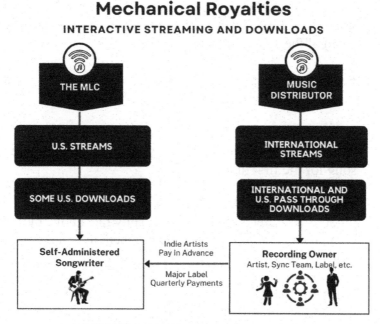

Mechanical Royalties
INTERACTIVE STREAMING AND DOWNLOADS

THE MLC

MUSIC DISTRIBUTOR

U.S. STREAMS

INTERNATIONAL STREAMS

SOME U.S. DOWNLOADS

INTERNATIONAL AND U.S. PASS THROUGH DOWNLOADS

Self-Administered Songwriter

Indie Artists Pay In Advance

Major Label Quarterly Payments

Recording Owner
Artist, Sync Team, Label, etc.

Mechanical Licensing for Physical Media like CD's and Vinyl as well as Digital Downloads

For independent artists and recording owners managing their own song releases, separating the mechanical royalties from the rest of the income generated from their recording can be a tedious task.

Therefore, self-administered songwriters are strongly advised to collect an advance on units sold, from 1,000-2,500 units at the time you provide the license. The licensee should come back and renew their license if sales exceed the original quantity.

For record labels with accounting systems in place, quarterly reports and payments should be sufficient to get your royalties.

Make sure your mechanical license gives you the right to audit the books of the label to make sure all units sold are properly paid out.

Understanding the First Use and Compulsory Rights

Before we get into the details of how to issue a mechanical license, we need to know that there are two types of mechanical licenses as defined by copyright law: first use and compulsory.

First Use: If a song has never been published before, the provisions of the Right of First Release come into effect for the copyright holder(s) of the song which include:

Exclusivity: First use is an "exclusive" license and can only be acquired directly from the copyright holder(s).

Release Authority: First use bestows the copyright holder(s) with the authority to determine who can or cannot publish the song for the first time.

Flexible Royalty Rate: First use provisions grant the copyright holder(s) the freedom to set the royalty rate above the compulsory statutory rate, allowing them to choose any royalty rate they desire.

Unrecoverable Loss: Once your song is published, the provisions of the first use are lost forever.

Artist/Co-writer Exemption: There is one circumstance where first use cannot be denied. If a co-writer of the song who is an artist wishes to publish the song, they may do so at any time. If the song is commercially released, the artist co-writer must obtain a mechanical license from their fellow co-writers and pay mechanical royalties.

Compulsory: Once your song has been published for the first time, it becomes subject to compulsory licensing, allowing anyone to release the song, provided it is licensed and the statutory royalty rate is paid to the copyright holder(s). You'll need to issue licenses directly to recording owners upon request.

First Use in the Real World

You'd be surprised at how many songs don't get cut because of first use. Sometimes a copyright holder will hold out for the "right" major label artist to record the song.

Or, say an artist you're writing with wants to hold onto the song and doesn't want someone else to cut the song first. Dicey! Just another reason to communicate with co-writers BEFORE writing the song, so you know where everyone stands.

Last, there's one more very important consideration of first use we want to discuss. A song is **"published"** when copies are distributed or when the work is publicly performed with the copyright owner's consent.

If a song is commercially released through a music distributor like CDBaby and it goes onto Spotify, obviously it's published.

If you and your co-writers write a song then later that day you sing it on TikTok, that's a public performance, and at that moment **all of the song's first use rights are lost.**

What about performing your song live at a local bar…and it's being live streamed on Instagram by you, or by an audience member without your permission? We'll have to opt for legal advice to further our understanding on this topic.

The Compulsory Mechanical Royalty Rate

Beginning in 2023, the NMPA, NSAI and others worked to raise the mechanical royalties for CDs, vinyl and digital downloads from 9.1 cents to 12 cents, a 32% increase. From now on, royalty rates will get a Cost-of-Living Adjustment (COLA) increase determined by the Consumer Price Index. **As of January 1, 2024, the rate is 12.40 cents.**

Exceptions to the Compulsory Royalty Rates

There are two circumstances when the royalty rate is lower than the statutory rate:

Controlled Compositions: Typically found in contracts between recording artists and major record labels, this clause reduces the statutory mechanical royalty rate that the label is obligated to pay for the reproduction and distribution of a musical composition, usually no lower than 75% of the statutory rate.

A controlled composition clause aims to control record label costs by specifying a reduced royalty rate, particularly beneficial when the artist is also the songwriter or holds music publishing rights.

Voluntary Royalty Rate Decrease: Songwriters and publishers may choose to lower the royalty rate for participation in a notable project.

For instance, we have a friend who's swing band accepted a reduced rate to be featured on a compilation album with Big Bad Voodoo Daddy and the Brian Setzer Orchestra.

In such cases, ensure your mechanical license includes a Most Favored Nations (MFN) clause to guarantee payment equal to or higher than other songwriters/publishers on the project. Check with a lawyer or publishing administrator on the language to add to your agreement.

When Should a Mechanical License Be Issued?

Mechanical royalties are owed to self-administered songwriters when their songs are reproduced as CDs, vinyl and digital downloads. Mechanical licenses are required:

> Whenever an artist wants to commercially release a song you wrote, they need to get a mechanical license from you.

> Whenever you want to release a song you co-wrote, you need to get a Mechanical License from your co-writers.

> Both of these instances are true even if the product is being given away for free or the project is for a non-profit.

How does it play out when someone wants to commercially release your song? A recording owner, usually an artist or label; comes directly to you wanting permission to record a song that you wrote. This can be a stranger or a co-writer.

> **Major Label:** If the artist is represented by a major label, they will most likely want to provide you with a mechanical licensing agreement that pays royalties on a quarterly basis. Nice, you don't have to do the work! But carefully review that the license has all the correct information. Have a lawyer look at it for you too if you don't understand anything!

> **Independent Artist:** If an indie artist wants to record your song, it is customary to issue a Mechanical License Agreement and collect royalties in advance for CDs, vinyl or digital downloads. Work with the artist to get all of the information you'll need which is highlighted in bold in the following sample Mechanical license.

What do you do when you want to commercially release a song you co-wrote?

> **Request a Mechanical License** from your co-writers (and their publishers). You'll need to provide them with all of the information they'll need which is highlighted in bold in the following Mechanical License. Be prepared to negotiate how many reproductions you'll need and pay the current mechanical royalty rate.

Consult a legal professional to ensure compliance with laws and to address the specific details of your situation.

SAMPLE: MECHANICAL LICENSE AGREEMENT

This Mechanical License Agreement (the "Agreement") is entered into by and between <u>Bill O'Hanlon of O Hanlon and O Hanlon Music</u>, hereinafter referred to as the "Licensor," and <u>Elvis Wesley</u>, hereinafter referred to as the "Licensee".

Licensee has advised Licensor, they wish to obtain a compulsory license to make and distribute phonorecords recordings of the copyrighted work listed below, under the compulsory license provision of Section 115 of the Copyright Act. Project information provided by Licensee is as follows:

DATE: January 1, 2024
SONG TITLE: Money, Money, Money
RECORD #01
ARTIST NAME: Elvis Wesley
LABEL: NewJackNashville
SONGWRITERS/PERCENTAGE: Bill O'Hanlon # 01006139110, 33.34%, Nancy Deckant, #511978444, 33.33%, Leslie Earl Bowe, #00241490684, 33.33%
PUBLISHERS/PERCENTAGE/PRO: O Hanlon and O Hanlon Music #00896183682, 33.34%, BMI, Nashville Cool Music #367539716, 33.33% BMI, LEB Music # 00182581262, 33.33% BMI
ISWC: (if digital release) T3012243771
RECORDING DURATION: 3:23
CONFIGURATION: Digital Downloads
ISRC:
UPC:
ROYALTY RATE: 100% of the current statutory rate.
RELEASE DATE: March 3, 2024

1) Upon signing this agreement, Licensee shall have all rights which are granted to, and all the obligations which are imposed upon, users of said copyrighted work under the compulsory license provision of the Copyright Act, after phonorecords and digital recordings of the copyrighted work have been distributed to the public in the United States under the authority of the copyright owner by another person, except that with respect to phonorecords thereof made and distributed hereunder;

2) Licensee will pay a fee of <u>$120</u> advance on sales of the first <u>1,000</u> copies of any configuration such as physical media and/or digital downloads manufactured for sale;

3) Licensee will account to Licensor quarterly, within 45 days (forty-five days) after the end of each calendar quarter, on the basis that the phonorecords/digital recordings are made and distributed. If an advance is paid against the first <u>1,000</u> units, no royalties will be paid until the advance has been recouped. Accounting on a quarterly basis is required by this license;

4) For such phonorecords made and distributed, the royalty shall be the Statutory rate in effect at the time the phonorecord is made;

5) This compulsory license covers and is limited to one particular recording of said copyrighted work as performed by the artist and on the phonorecord number listed above; and this compulsory license does not supersede nor in any way affect any prior agreements now in effect respecting phonorecords of said copyrighted work;

6) Licensor agrees to include writer and publisher credits within graphics and imagery displayed with regard to all reproductions distributed;

7) Licensee is entitled to distribute up to 100 (one hundred) promotional copies for which royalties do not need to be paid;

8) In the event Licensee fails to account to us and pay royalties as herein provided for, said publisher(s) may give written notice to you that, unless the default is remedied within 30 days of your receipt of the notice, this compulsory license will be automatically terminated. Such termination shall render either the making or the distribution, or both, of all phonorecords for which royalties have not been paid, actionable as acts of infringement under, and fully subject to the remedies provided by, the Copyright Act;

9) Parties may assign its rights under this agreement, and it shall be binding upon the heirs, legal representatives, successors, and assigns of the parties. Licensee agrees to inform Licensor in writing of any assignment and provide details regarding the assigns involved in the transfer of rights;

10) Parties agree to indemnify each other, along with successors, licensees, and assignees, from all claims, liabilities, damages, costs, or expenses arising from any breach of representations, warranties, or agreements made under this agreement:

11) This Agreement shall be governed by and construed in accordance with the laws of the State of Tennessee. Any action under this Agreement shall be brought in Davidson County, whose courts shall have exclusive jurisdiction over any dispute arising here from;

12) This Agreement shall be granted world-wide;

13) This Agreement constitutes the entire understanding between the parties and supersedes all prior negotiations and understandings;

14) This Agreement may be executed in separate counterparts, each of which shall be deemed as original, but all of which taken together shall constitute one and the same instrument.

15) Label Copy should include the following: Songwriters: Bill O'Hanlon, Nancy Deckant, Leslie Earl Bowe: Publishers O'Hanlon and O'Hanlon Music (BMI), Nashville Cool Music (BMI), LEB Music (BMI)

ACCEPTED AND AGREED:

Licensee: NewJackNashville
Signature/Date

Phone, Email Address

Licensor: Bill O'Hanlon of O Hanlon and O Hanlon Music
Signature/Date
Phone, Email Address
Mail check payable to: O Hanlon and O Hanlon

How To Get a Mechanical License for A Cover Song

While we are not covering how to offer mechanical licenses for your songs through Harry Fox, a big part of being an artist is commercially releasing cover songs. Here's how to license covers.

After a song has been granted first use and commercially released for sale, anyone can record and release the song. You'll need to obtain a compulsory mechanical license directly from all of the publisher(s) of the song or from a mechanical rights organization such as:

> **Harry Fox Agency (HFA)** issues physical and download mechanical compulsory licenses for units of 2,500 or more.

> **Songfile (part of HFA)** and EasySong.com issue mechanical compulsory licenses for projected units of 2,500 or less.

Licensing songs from these organizations can be straightforward. Just go to their website to start the process. The biggest issue is finding the organization that represents the song you want to cover.

If you find the song when you do a search on their website, you're good to go. But if the song is not there, you may have to do a "custom" license, or go directly to all of the publishers of the song.

Direct from Publisher (Custom) Licenses

Custom licenses are expensive, take time and there is no guarantee that the license will be granted, so plan accordingly!

1) First use (not compulsory) songs.

2) If you want changes to the lyrics or melody.

3) Medleys and parodies.

4) Release for any public purpose (other than a private party), like performance or karaoke, etc.

5) License an international song or theatrical productions.

6) License for YouTube videos.

7) Lyrics.

Five Million Streams: The Right Time to Go Big-Time!

This book **does not** include information on two important sources of mechanical licensing revenue used for widely-popular songs usually released by major labels:

1) How to become a registered publisher with Harry Fox Agency (HFA) to authorize them to issue mechanical licenses on your behalf of your songs.

2) When your song has low international streaming and downloading activity there's no need to employ a publishing administrator to collect international (neighboring rights) mechanical royalties for recordings of your song.

However, there is a right time to act!

When one of your songs reaches the five million stream mark, consider listing your song on Harry Fox or securing a publishing administrator's services to collect international royalties and issue mechanical licenses.

Checklist for Mechanical Royalties

1) Contact an entertainment lawyer to get a mechanical license. Talk over the fine points to be sure you understand every nuance!

2) When someone wants to record your song, issue a mechanical license. Use the mechanical license as a guide and see Chapter 10 Your Publisher Playbook for step-by-step instructions.

3) Sign up for the Mechanical License Collective (MLC) to get your U.S. mechanical royalties for streaming and downloads.

a) How-To-Videos at: https://www.nashvillecool.com/press

4) Join The MLC https://www.themlc.com.

    a) Set up your account and payment information.

    b) Claim existing songs released to the public.

    c) Register new songs not already in The MLC.

5) If one of your songs achieves 5 million streams, consider hiring a publishing administrator and/or joining Harry Fox as a publisher.

6) Go to these organizations to license cover songs:

    a) Songfile https://www.songfile.com and EasySong for fewer than 2500.

    b) HFA for 2500 and above: https://www.harryfox.com

Chapter 3 charts and download sample mechanical license at https://www.nashvillecool.com/tsg

4. Master Royalties for Recording Owners

Master royalties, also master recording royalties, refers to payments made to the owner of the recording whenever the song is reproduced as CDs, vinyl, digital downloads and streams.

First, let's begin with this flowchart, and then we'll break down how royalties make their way to recording owners.

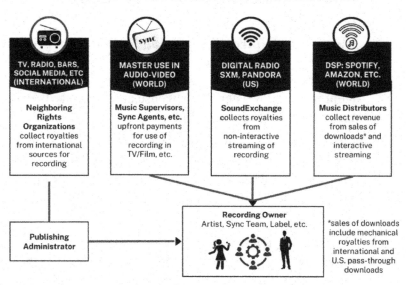

How Master Royalties are Generated in the U.S.

1) **Release by Music Distributor:** Owners of recordings, often artists, record labels and sync teams, release singles and albums through music distributors such as DistroKid, TuneCore, CDBaby, etc.

   These distributors disseminate music to digital streaming platforms (DSPs) like Spotify, Apple Music, etc. Owners then receive royalties whenever the recording is streamed, downloaded, or sold in physical formats like CDs and vinyl from online stores.

2) **Recording Digital Performance Royalties** are generated by the recording for plays on non-interactive streaming platforms like Internet radio, Pandora, Cable/Satellite radio and paid to the owner of the master by SoundExchange.

3) **Physical Sales:** Artists directly sell CDs and vinyl plus digital downloads at live performances or through their websites and other venues.

4) **Master Use "Upfront" Licensing Royalties** are generated by recordings when they are used in movies, TV shows, commercials, videos, and games. A music supervisor or sync agent issues a "Master Use" license and a royalty is paid directly to the recording owner.

   Side note: If your recording is featured in a "union" commercial and recorded with union players; the vocalist and musicians may earn royalties through SAG-AFTRA. Performers on the recording are not required to join the union. Get the details at SAG-AFTRA.

5) **Neighboring Rights Organizations** funnel international master royalties generated by the recording back to the recording owners when their songs are played on terrestrial radio, TV, bars in foreign countries or licensed by artists. Employ a publishing administrator to collect royalties on your song's behalf once it's clear royalties are being generated.

Who owns the master? Well, usually whoever paid for it. However, the details depend on the contracts and agreements among the parties involved.

There can be many people involved who might claim ownership of the master if you don't have a clear agreement in place before the recording process starts. Some key stakeholders of recordings might be:

- **Record Labels:** Record labels typically invest in the production, distribution, and promotion of recordings and therefore own the master. Alternatively, artists may have already paid for the production of their masters. In this case, the label will negotiate for the right to license and/or own some percentage of the master.

- **Recording Artists/Performers:** The individuals who perform the music have rights in the recording if they pay for the master. In some cases, these "master rights" may be assigned to a record label.

- **Producers** sometimes negotiate a percentage of the master, called "points". The artist might give the producer 5% which is considered 5 points, of the income generated by the income. Some producers will want to share in the ownership "master rights" of the recording. Also, producers may even ask for some of the song's publishing rights, to be able to give a better deal on the costs of the recording. Songwriters might even leverage their publishing rights to attract a producer they otherwise couldn't secure without giving up a portion of those rights.

- **Studio Musicians, Vocalists, Mixing Engineer, Mastering Engineer** who perform and work on the recording may negotiate for some percentage ownership of the master.

- **Songwriters:** While the copyright for the musical composition is distinct from the composition, songwriters may have some rights in the recording if they have negotiated these rights.

- **Sync Songwriting Teams**: Often comprised of songwriters, artists and producers who strategically target sync opportunities, will pay for the recording to maximize earnings and make their song easy to clear.

- **Publishers:** More often these days publishers also invest in the production, distribution, and promotion of recordings for the Artist/Writers signed to their company.

Some situations are complex! You may have written a song with two other songwriters. Then the three of you hire a producer, musicians and a vocalist to create a great version of the song. The producer may hire a mixer or mastering engineer.

Any type of sharing deal is okay as long as all the parties agree and there is a clear, written and signed agreement in place.

Paper Up: Work For Hire

In the music industry, it is a common practice to use "Work For Hire" (WFH) agreements in recording situations. This defines the terms of engagement between the recording owner and musicians and vocalists who performed on the song.

Always get a WFH from the producer and the vocalist. See Chapter 11 for a sample agreement.

How the SoundExchange Royalty Pie is Divided

Now that we have a firm grasp on the details of master ownership, let's take a look at the distribution of royalties by SoundExchange.

These details may evolve as SoundExchange periodically updates its policies and procedures.

Rights Holders: SoundExchange pays royalties to both featured and non-featured artists, and the recording owner. Featured artists are typically the performers or bands whose names are credited on the recording, while non-featured artists might include session musicians or backup singers.

50-45-5 Split: SoundExchange divides the royalties as follows: Under the law, 45 percent of performance royalties are paid directly to the featured artists on a recording, and 5 percent are paid to a fund for non-featured artists. The other 50 percent of the performance royalties are paid to the rights owner of the sound recording.

Direct Payment to Artists: SoundExchange pays featured artists directly, bypassing the record label. This is a notable distinction from some other types of royalties, where payments typically go through the record label.

Non-Featured Performers: Non-featured performers, such as session musicians or background singers, receive their share through the SoundExchange Letters of Direction (LOD).

Download the LOD from SoundExchange and follow their directions.

Checklist for Master Royalties

1) Distribute your song(s) for sale on digital platforms and streaming services, use one of these platforms: DistroKid, TuneCore, CDBaby, etc. See Chapter 6 for detailed information.

2) Register your Phonogram ℗ copyright when your song is released to the public. See Chapter 5 for details.

3) If you own any portion of the master, after the song is released to the public, register it with SoundExchange to gather digital streaming royalties for "non-interactive" streaming performances.

   a) Join at https://www.soundexchange.com/,

   b) Create a new account and add your payment details.

   c) Register your ownership percentage as songs are released to the public.

4) Watch your PRO statement to understand what songs have traction. Engage a publishing administrator to collect royalties on your behalf if your songs are getting millions of plays outside of the U.S.

Chapter 4 charts at https://www.nashvillecool.com/tsg

5. Copyrighting Your Songs in the U.S.

When you write a song it is automatically copyrighted if you document it; either in writing or through audio or video recording. No need to formally copyright; your music just does its own legal abracadabra!

Many non-professional songwriters feel they need to copyright their songs because they're worried someone will steal it. But those of us who do songwriting for a living know that it is hard to get anyone with any major success to listen to our song, much less want to steal it! Not saying that no one has ever heard a song and not copied parts of it or the title.

In a town full of songwriters like Nashville, professional writers exercise caution in choosing the time and place to unveil new songs with fresh titles and innovative concepts aiming to avoid potential copyright infringement cases.

> A good example is "I Drive Your Truck" co-written by Jessi Alexander, Connie Harrington, and Jimmy Yeary. Before the song was released to the public, Nancy heard Jimmy Yeary sing it at the Bluebird Café.
>
> Jimmy introduced the song by saying that his publisher was finally letting him sing the song in public because Lee Brice had recorded it and the song was making its way to radio. The song went on to win Song of Year due in part to its fresh title, innovative concept, and ability to make most any listener cry!

Formal Copyright Protections

Registering your copyright through the Library of Congress grants the copyright holder exclusive authority over pivotal actions which control how a created work is used. These rights form the cornerstone of intellectual property protection:

- The right of first use and to set the royalty rate on the first use.
- To reproduce.
- To distribute.
- To display or perform works publicly.
- To create derivative works.

Registering your copyright with the Library of Congress grants you the right to claim specific "statutory damages" in a court copyright infringement case, provided you can demonstrate authorship and legitimate entitlement to the copyright.

Statutory damages are a set amount of compensation by law without having to prove the specific financial harm caused by the infringement.

Furthermore, if you can establish that the copyright infringement has harmed the value or potential income of your song, you may be eligible for additional damages beyond the statutory rate.

When (and when not to) Register Your Copyright

You'll need to weigh the cost of copyrighting against the potential benefits especially if you have a large catalog of songs.

Professional writers wait until they know those songs are published before they register their songs with the copyright office. Why? Because they write many songs and it's expensive to copyright them all. **But don't wait too long!**

Many creators and publishers put off registering their songs until their work gains significant success. Waiting risks potential losses of thousands of dollars, complicates legal actions and limits statutory damages from $250 to $150,000 per infringement

According to Barry Shrum, ESQ www.shrumdisney.com, timely copyright registration is crucial for protecting creative works and sets two important time frames to remember.

3-Month Post-Publication Period: Once your song is published, you have three months to register your work to ensure statutory damages. If you miss this time frame, you'll need to prove "actual damages" in court.

5-Year Window: If you register within five years of publishing, it makes ownership clear in court and simplifies the legal process. Missing this time frame puts the burden of proof on the copyright owner (you), and the court decides.

How To Prove You Wrote a Song

One of the simplest things you can do to prove you own a song is to register your song with your PRO, keep records of your writing appointments and hold on to drafts of lyrics and recordings.

How Long Does a Copyright Last?

As a general rule in the U.S., for songs created after January 1, 1978, copyright protection lasts for the life of the last surviving author plus 70 years, then the song becomes "public domain".

What is Public Domain?

After the song goes out of copyright, generally, it enters the public domain and the original songwriter(s) no longer collect royalties. But again, this is a complex subject, and you should always get legal advice to clarify the status of a song you want to record or that you wrote.

What Is Not Copyrightable?

According to copyright law, you can't copyright a title!

How To Register a Copyright for Your Song

If and when you do decide to register the copyright of your song, go to the Library of Congress at copyright.gov. As of current publication these are the rates:

-$45 online for a single composition written by a solo songwriter.
-$65 online for multiple songs by the same solo songwriter.

-$85 online for a group of works as long as all of the songs are written by the same songwriters.
-$65 online for a recording.
-$125 by mail for either the composition or recording.

The copyright office will provide a copyright certificate after you complete the process.

Checklist For Copyrighting Your Song

1) Keep records of the writing process. Any notes or idea recordings, rough work tapes, early demos, etc. Make sure to date everything.

2) Register your song with your PRO right after you've finished it. The date you register it will be part of the proof of when the song was created and part of the informal evidence that you wrote the song.

3) If and when the song is recorded, register your song with the copyright through the Library of Congress within 3 months of it being commercially released. https://www.copyright.gov/

   a) If you own 100% of the recording, you'll pay for the copyright yourself.

   b) If you co-own the recording with others; split the cost proportionally according to your ownership percentage.

4) You'll need the lyrics and recording during the copyright registration. But the recording can be as simple as you singing into your phone and retrieving the mp3.

5) Keep your copyright registrations with your will. Your registered copyright can be handed down to your family and friends just like any other piece of property.

Chapter 6 charts at https://www.nashvillecool.com/tsg

6. How Music Distributors, DSPs & Social Media Boost Royalties

When it's time to commercially release your song, you'll go through a music distributor who will make your music accessible to a global audience through digital music stores and streaming services.

Each music distributor has its own unique fee structure and suite of services. recording owners should carefully consider their needs and goals when selecting a digital distribution service.

Some widely used music distributors are listed below with the first three being most popular.

1) **DistroKid:** Known for its simplicity and affordable pricing with a flat annual fee for unlimited uploads but lots of extra costs. No fee on royalties, all the money you make is yours.

2) **TuneCore:** Offers distribution services along with additional features like music publishing administration.

3) **CD Baby:** Provides distribution services, and like TuneCore, it also offers music publishing services. Only service we know of that keeps your song on the platform even if you let your account expire.

4) **LANDR:** Offers distribution services and is also known for its AI-based music mastering services.

5) **Repost by SoundCloud:** 80/20 split on revenue. $30/year for unlimited releases and no extra cost if you want to release songs under other artist names. Very few, if any, extra costs.

6) **Amuse:** Known for its free distribution model, allowing artists to distribute their music without upfront costs; they also act as a label for some artists.

7) **Stem:** Focuses on helping artists split and manage revenue among collaborators efficiently.

8) **Bandcamp:** Bandcamp and Bandzoogle are platforms/websites that allow artists to sell music directly to fans. You can set your own prices and keep a larger portion of the revenue compared to other platforms. They also offer tools for promoting your music and building your fanbase.

9) **AWAL (Artists Without a Label):** Known for working with emerging indie artists and offering more personalized services.

10) **ONErpm:** Offers distribution services and provides features such as YouTube monetization and rights management. Known for working with emerging indie artists.

11) **Symphonic Distribution:** Provides distribution along with various additional services like neighboring rights collection. Known for working with emerging indie artists.

12) **The Orchard**: Provides distribution along with various additional services like neighboring rights collection. Known for working with emerging independent artists.

Digital Service Providers (DSPs)

Music distributors help increase the chances of getting your song on DSP playlists by providing accurate metadata, such as the song title, artist name, and album artwork.

They can also provide tools and services to help promote the music, such as social media and email marketing, which can help increase fan engagement and plays on the platform.

The good news is streaming services make music accessible to everyone. The bad news is, it's challenging for artists to distinguish themselves and gain recognition, plus these services pay very low royalty rates to songwriters and publishers.

Despite this, music distributors have made music accessible not only on DSPs and digital stores.

The key players are:

1) **Spotify** is an interactive music, podcast, and video streaming service with millions of songs. It is currently the largest streaming platform in the world.

2) **Apple Music** is Apple's interactive streaming service with access to over 50 million songs. Apple Music reigns in second place in popularity around the world.

3) **Amazon Music** is an online streaming service and music store with more than 2 million songs. Listeners easily play any song on the platform through echo devices in their homes.

4) **Tidal** is a subscription-based music, podcast, and video streaming service that features high-fidelity sound, hi-def video, curated playlists, and original content.

5) **Deezer** is a streaming platform with more than 56 million tracks, originating in France and now available in over 180 countries.

6) **Pandora** is a major music and podcast discovery platform, providing a highly-personalized listening experience to more than 70 million users.

7) **SoundCloud:** Focuses on helping artists identify their top fans based on their listening and enables artists to message their fans directly. Fan-powered royalties are calculated differently than other services. Each listener's subscription and advertising revenue is distributed among the artists they actually listen to, rather than being pooled like other DSPs.

Music-Infused Micro-Content on Social Media

Music distributors now facilitate seamless music delivery to many social media platforms.

Utilizing micro-content, such as short videos, stories, GIFs, and memes, is a popular strategy for businesses and individuals to enhance brand visibility and engagement on social media.

If your music distributor allows you to add your own music to social media sites. Do it!

Every time your song is played on social media in a post, reel or video, you earn performance royalties for your composition.

Music Distribution on Social Media

Make sure you check whatever boxes your music distributor provides that allow your music to be offered on these social media sites.

1) **TikTok:** TikTok is known for its extensive music library that users can use to add soundtracks to their short videos. TikTok allows users to search for specific songs, browse popular tracks, and discover trending sounds to enhance their content.

2) **Facebook:** Facebook provides a music feature that allows users to add music to their stories and posts. Similar to Instagram, users can choose from a variety of tracks and even use your own music to personalize their content with music.

3) **Instagram:** Instagram offers users the ability to add music to their reels. Users can choose from a vast library of songs, search for specific tracks, and even use your own music.

4) **Snapchat:** Snapchat allows users to add music to their Snaps through its Recordings feature. Users can select from a library of licensed music to accompany their photos and videos.

5) **YouTube Shorts:** YouTube Shorts is a short-form video platform within the YouTube app. Users can access a music library to add soundtracks to their Shorts, enhancing the overall appeal of their brief videos.

Performance Royalties from Facebook and Instagram

Your songs can earn royalties through video content, whether you uploaded it or not. Enabling ads, known as "monetization," on platforms like YouTube and Meta's Facebook and Instagram can generate income.

Chapter 6 charts at https://www.nashvillecool.com/tsg

7. Royalties from Direct Licensing

What Is Direct Licensing?

There are performance royalties that completely bypass PROs and flow directly to songwriters, publishers, and recording owners, if they are aware of them and make the effort to get them.

Some of these royalties can be obtained simply by joining organizations, while others require actively seeking out organizations that facilitate direct licensing between songwriters and companies.

New Performance Royalties from Streaming

Companies that use music as a part of their world-wide accessible platforms like TikTok (social media), Peloton (work out) and Roblox (games) opened new avenues for music use, but this also created challenges for songwriters without clear regulations and compensation.

Fortunately, laws are evolving, and several organizations have stepped in to ensure the royalties rightfully due to songwriters and publishers are paid.

The National Music Publishers Association (NMPA) is a trade association that represents music publishers and songwriters in the U.S. which is currently headed up by David Israelite.

Alongside Bart Herbison, the Executive Director of the Nashville Songwriters Association International (NSAI) and others, the NMPA lobbied Congress on behalf of songwriters and publishers helping to usher in the MMA laws which raised royalty rates and clarified regulations.

Thereafter the NMPA began negotiating licensing agreements with companies like Snapchat, "X", Peloton, Roblox and more to ensure songwriters get paid when their music is used in their products and services.

These royalties bypass the PROs and flow directly from the NMPA to their members who opt into licensing agreements negotiated by the NMPA.

> Amid the pandemic, Nancy opted-in to licensing agreements from the NMPA and started receiving royalty checks from $175 to $2,800 from companies of various platforms. No doubt, this is the easiest money she's ever made as a songwriter and publisher!

All songwriters currently actively involved in publishing their music are welcome to join The NMPA (check their requirements):

- Membership fee: $100 per year. They have a member sign up/renew period every year. Get on their email list and they will let you know when enrollment is open.

- No song registration hassle – just opt-in to agreements as the company emails you.

- Visit: https://www.nmpa.org.

Music Reports (MRI)

MRI manages digital licenses and collects streaming royalties from platforms like Facebook, Amazon Music Videos, Instagram, TikTok, etc.

MRI administers "voluntary" licenses for companies using music as a part of their product and offers publishers the opportunity to participate and receive royalties by opting in.

> Let's demonstrate the process. Nancy registered as a publisher on Music Reports and chose to participate in an agreement

between MRI and Twitter. Nancy recently got an email from MRI telling her it's time to "opt-in" to the yearly license.

According to the agreement, Twitter will remit a monthly amount to MRI for utilizing music on their platform. MRI then distributes this sum among all the publishers. Given the size of Nancy's publishing company, she will receive a modest check. Nancy signed the opt-in agreement. Five minutes, and it's done!

The details:

- Joining Music Reports Inc. is free.

- Songwriters can join.

- Opt-In: No song registration hassle. Just opt-in to agreements as the company emails you.

- Visit: https://www.musicreports.com.

Overhead Radio

Overhead Radio involves direct licensing of songs to venues such as malls, bars, airports, etc.

In this arrangement, the licensee pays the self-administered songwriter directly for use of their composition and recording, and no PRO royalties are involved.

Websites like Songtradr.com and RadioSparx.com offer overhead radio opportunities. Go to their website to learn more.

Black Box Royalties

Black Box Royalties, also known as "unallocated," "unmatched," or "unclaimed" royalties, arise from incomplete or inaccurate data, preventing rightful copyright holders from claiming them.

These royalties originate from digital music services such as streaming platforms and download stores. If unclaimed within three years, they are subsequently distributed to major labels and publishers. Here's what to do:

To dodge the black box drama, make sure you register your songs with your PRO within three years of their release.

Thanks to MMA laws, The MLC has a mission to track down the rightful owners of those elusive royalties. A staggering $432 million recently landed in The MLC's coffers from the DSPs and online stores.

The MLC is still working through exactly how they will disperse these royalties. In the future, it may be as easy as checking your account. Those once-missing royalties might just make a surprise appearance!

Print Royalties

Print Royalties are generated by the composition for use of lyrics on MusicNotes, LyricFind or wherever you find lyrics.

Musicnotes.com sells sheet music. They work with publishers and licensing agencies to offer sheet music for various songs; and they have a submission process for self-administered songwriters. Follow their guidelines for submission. This may involve providing information about the song, proof of ownership, and perhaps a sample of the sheet music.

Checklist: Direct Licensing, Print, Black Box Royalties

1) Join the NMPA: https://www.nmpa.org.

2) Join Music Reports https://www.musicreports.com.

3) Sign up to The MLC and you'll get periodic updates on how to claim "unclaimed" black box royalties.

4) Check out overhead radio on RadioSparx https://www.radiosparx.com.

5) Check out overhead radio on Songtradr https://www.songtradr.com.

6) Music Notes https://www.musicnotes.com

Chapter 7 charts at https://www.nashvillecool.com/tsg

8. Sync Licensing

Synchronization. sometimes shortened to "sync" or "synch," is the practice of matching music with audio-visual content.

Sync really is the new superhero on the music business mountain top. With streaming platforms being stingy with royalties, songwriters and publishers are searching for new sources of income. Who needs spare change from Spotify when your tunes can be rocking out on the silver screen? Some people even make a full-time living through sync licensing.

Sync Licensing Essentials: Composition vs. Master Use Rights

The term "sync licenses" encompasses two key elements: the synchronization right, which pertains to the use of the composition, and the master use right, which relates to the recording in audio-visual media. These are sometimes called "sides" in sync license offers and briefs.

- **Synchronization Right for the Composition:** This refers to the permission granted by the copyright owner of the musical composition (usually the music publisher or songwriter) to synchronize that composition with visual media, such as a film, TV show, commercial, or video game.

- **Master Use Right for the Recording:** This involves obtaining permission from the owner of the recording to use a specific recording of the musical composition in synchronization with visual media.

When a filmmaker, producer, or any party wishes to incorporate a particular song into audiovisual media, they need to secure both the synchronization right for the composition and the "master use" of the recording, to ensure that they have the legal right to use underlying composition and recording.

Sync Royalties

There are three distinct royalties for sync licensing:

1) **Synchronization (Sync) Licensing Fees** are generated by the composition when it is used in audio-visual media like movies, TV shows, commercials, games, etc. This money flows to self-administered songwriters by way of licenses issued by music supervisors, sync agents, music libraries, etc.

2) **Master Use Licensing Fees** are generated by the recording when it is used in audio-visual media like movies, TV shows, commercials, games, etc. This money flows to self-administered songwriters by way of licenses issued by music supervisors, sync agents, music libraries, etc.

3) **Sync-related Back End Royalties** are generated by the composition when audio-visual media like movies, TV shows, commercials, games, etc. are aired. These royalties flow to self-administered songwriters by way of their PRO.

   Royalties from movies are exclusively collected when the film is broadcast on television and streaming services. It's noteworthy that the U.S. stands as the sole country not paying performance royalties for movie theater screenings.

How Much Are Sync Placements Worth?

The composition is paid the same amount as the recording. Earnings from placements are influenced by many factors.

- The visual media: social media to a major motion picture.

- The duration of usage, from a one-time use to perpetuity.

- The production budget of the film and the music budget.

- The geographical region of use: local to global audience.

- The popularity of the artist.

- The length of the audio segment.

- The manner of usage, background music vs. opening or closing credits.

Tips for Negotiating the Upfront Fee

According to our fellow publishers who work with music supervisors, there's a short-hand involved in negotiations. Suppose the music supervisor expresses interest in using 1 minute and 10 seconds of your song in a scene and offers $1500. If you counter with a request for $3000, they might respond with a slightly higher offer. If they say their **final offer** is $1750, accept it! The conversation is likely to end very abruptly if you don't.

On the other hand, **until** you hear a phrase like "this is a one-time offer" or "this is our best and final offer," negotiations remain open.

Writing For Sync

Writing songs for sync is different than writing for yourself or artists. Lyrics should evoke emotions and not be too specific so they don't interfere with the visual images in the film.

Most sync placements require high-quality recordings. Demos or rough recordings are rarely used. Most music supervisors, usually the curators of the music for the film, want songs that sound like they could be on the radio today with fresh sonic landscapes and artists with distinctive vocals unless they tell you they are looking for something that is retro. If they provide a reference track, get as close as possible without infringing on someone else's song.

Getting Your Sync Ducks in A Row

Everything in the sync industry moves fast. We have had briefs (descriptions of songs needed) that come in and are needed to be sent back in an hour. That means you need to have everything "clear" and ready to submit or you will miss out on opportunities.

Sync professionals may want to following and you really need to be ready with all of it!

- A signed split sheet with all your co-writer's information, their PRO, percentage of ownership of the song, contact information, who has the right to say "Yes" to a sync deal.

- Work for hire agreements.

- A high-quality full mix.

- The instrumental.

- The vocal STEM.

- Optionally be ready with all of the stems of the recording: stereo files of each track or groups of tracks used in the recording, main vocal, harmony vocals, background vocals, drums, bass, guitars, pianos/keys etc.

One Stop Agreements

You must own the rights to the composition and recording (or have permission to pitch it) and be able to sign a licensing deal on behalf of all the necessary parties.

When you write and record songs especially for tv/film, get an agreement from your co-writers and recording owner allowing any writer to say "yes" to a licensing offer.

This is often called an administration or "one stop" agreement. It is an administration agreement because it specifies who can administer (or issue) the license. And it is called a "one stop" agreement if the person who wants to license the song only needs to go to one person or one place for a license. View a sample agreement in Chapter 11.

If you record a cover song, those can almost **never** be one stop. Whoever licenses the song will need to get your permission to use the recording, and also get permission from the composition's songwriters and publisher(s).

Music supervisors, sync agents and music libraries prefer one stop songs because they can make licensing deals quick and easy. This is one way that self-administered songwriters have an advantage over writers signed to publishers and especially large publishing companies.

Recording owners, especially artists, who release music through CDBaby, TuneCore, SongTrust, etc. need to be aware that these kinds of publishing administration agreements, can stand in your way of your song being a one stop.

The Music Business Players in Sync

To get opportunities for sync placements and licensing deals, connect to the following:

1) **Music supervisors** curate music for use in TV shows, movies, commercials, promos, ads, commercials, etc. They find the music that fits the show's scenes and fits within the budget of the project. They usually work with directors, movie/TV producers, show runners, etc. – the people who make the final decision about budgets and which music will be used.

2) **Sync agents** are individuals, often times publishers, who have connections to music supervisors and other companies looking for music for their audio-visual projects. Sync agents represent your music in exchange for a share of the upfront sync licensing fee and sometimes your publishing income for placements they obtain on your behalf.

3) **Sync agencies** are either small or large companies employing one or more sync agents. These agencies find projects requiring music and serve as representatives for songwriters, pitching songs for licensing opportunities, and negotiating licensing deals and payment amounts.

4) **Music libraries** are companies with a large number of songs that are instantly available for licensing. Their libraries often include pieces of music that are not even whole songs, but shorter snippets of instrumental tracks, called cues. If you listen closely to many TV shows or movies, you'll hear these cues. Because libraries aim to be comprehensive, they may be the easiest to approach to get your songs signed. Also, because they have so many songs, they may not focus on yours like smaller agencies might.

5) **Ad agencies** mostly solicit music for advertisement and company branding.

6) **Custom music production companies** (or "houses" as they are often called) have songwriters, vocalists, and producers on staff who can create music specifically for projects, usually turning that music around, with suggested revisions, pretty quickly.

Sync Agent Contracts

When one of the players in sync wants to represent your song and pitch it for licensing opportunities, they will offer you a contract with most of these elements:

Grants permission to represent your song, negotiate licenses, and collect licensing fees. Facilitates distribution of licensing fees to you and other master recording owners.

Term Duration: Ranges from 1 year to perpetuity (forever).

Exclusive Representation: Prohibits signing other contracts or pitching the song for sync opportunities during the contract. Exclusivity usually applies only to sync opportunities not to artist cuts.

Non-Exclusive Representation: Allows signing and pitching of your song under other non-exclusive contracts.

Both Exclusive and Non-Exclusive Arrangements Allow: Artist recording of your song. Release of your recorded version for streaming or on vinyl. Live performances of the song.

Financial Split: Varies from 20% to 50% of the upfront licensing income. Sync agent/agency/library may receive a percentage of your publishing income from obtained placements if they place your song.

Getting Sync Placements

You might be wondering, "How do I get my songs to these sync players?" That is beyond the scope of this book and it is a big topic.

Like most areas of music, immersing yourself in the topic, reading books, taking courses, attending webinars and talking to others who have succeeded in the sync arena are good first steps.

Relationships and connections, like in most arenas of life and business, are so critical. A good starting place is to go to events where you can meet music supervisors like: Durango Songwriter Festival, Nashville Film Festival, Sync Summit, Taxi Road Rally.

What is Song Re-titling in Sync?

"Re-titling" refers to the practice of assigning a new title to a song that has already been created and published. This new title is used specifically for the purpose of licensing the music for synchronization in visual media such as TV shows, films, commercials, or video games.

The primary reason for re-titling is to differentiate the licensed version of the song from the original version. This helps in tracking and accounting for royalties associated with the licensed use of the music. And the re-titling sync agent or music library will get paid on the songs that they get placed into projects.

Here's how it typically works:

1) **Original Title:** The composer or songwriter has an original title for their song. Let's say Jingle Punks wants "Plus One" to be in their catalog.

2) **Retitled Version:** Jingle Punks gives the song a unique title, Plus One_JP" and registers the song with your PRO. You'll now see "Plus One" and "Plus One_JP in your list of songs with Jingle Punks being the publisher on "Plus One_JP."

3) **Tracking and Royalties:** Royalties generated from the licensed use of the "Plus One_JP' version are then distributed to the appropriate parties.

A Word of Caution on Re-titling!

Re-titling is a common practice in the sync licensing industry but there's a downside - so be smart about this!

Music supervisors get very uncomfortable when they receive the same song under 10 different titles, from 10 different sync professionals. For the music supervisor, it's about ownership of the song, and who can most easily get to "Yes" without a legal conflict.

We suggest that once your song is retitled, don't place that song in many other places. Find other uses for it. It can go to overhead music licensors. Maybe it can be an artist cut or go on a soundtrack. Alternatively, you can write a new song close to that vibe so you can have a song like that in your catalog to pitch. Make sense?

Maximizing Music Placement with Metadata

Metadata, also referred to as meta tags, functions akin to keywords we employ when searching online.

For instance: "Best Chinese Restaurant in Des Moines" or "Day Hikes in Cornwall." These are keywords and tags that can be added to your music tracks when they are released online or pitched for musical artists or sync placement.

At times, individuals who receive songs may listen long after it was sent, and may forget who sent it, who wrote it, or how to contact the writers or people associated with the song. This oversight could result in a missed opportunity for a cut or placement.

Publishers and sync agents manage extensive catalogs of songs, and the use of meta tags and metadata becomes essential for efficient searches.

When pitching songs for artists, specific parameters are often provided, such as the requirement for an up-tempo female country pop song or a ballad. Meta tags streamline searches, enabling easy location of specific songs based on criteria like co-writers, genre, lyrics, or other variables.

> While writing this book, Nancy had an opportunity to pitch songs to a successful country artist looking for female pop-country songs. Despite the short notice, metadata searching allowed her to quickly identify suitable songs from Bill, who sent them along. The artist ended up selecting three of Bill's songs that Nancy pitched, all fitting exactly what the artist was looking for.

All of us have heard stories of someone wanting to record or license a song but having to give up on the idea due to the inability to find who sent or pitched the song.

Here is a note from a prominent music supervisor to those of us who he sends pitch opportunities for TV, movies, commercials, and video games to:

> "Happy Friday everyone! I want to send a quick reminder of how important metadata is. Without metadata, we don't know who the song belongs to. It's happened a few times where we want to forward a song, but can't because it has no metadata."

METADATA MATTERS!!! **At the very least**, *include your name, email, and phone. We want you to win! Give metadata a shot.*

The 411 on Metadata

Metadata can potentially include:

- Writers' names and contact information.
- Publishers' names and contact information.
- Beats per minute (BPM).
- Instrumentation (guitar, bass, piano, drums, percussion, organ, strings, synth, etc.)
- Type of vocal (male, female, background, harmonies, vocalese, scat, gang vocals, etc.)
- Genre.
- Lyrics.
- Lyric content and topics.
- Feel or mood of the song.
- Songs or artists this song "may be like".
- Whether or not the song is licensable as a "one stop" or "easy clear" meaning there's a publisher but they are readily available for approval and signatures.
- Whether the song has been recorded and released or is a pre-release scheduled for the future.
- Any special minority/marginalized status of writers/producers, vocalists (BIPOC; LGTBQIA+; AAPI).

- Geographical information for anyone involved in the writing, singing, or production of the song (Canada-based, Chicago-based artist, Swedish producer, etc.)

- Language of the song (English, Korean, etc.)

Metadata Security 101: Choosing the Right File Sharing Method

Sharing music while preserving the text you've added to the inside of your file is sometimes a problem. Sync professionals request their preferred format (320 kbps mp3, wav, aiff) and data has a way of not showing up in the file!

Metadata sticks to mp3 files very well. But if you send a wav file with metadata by email, the metadata will be missing when the file is opened. It even gets stripped out from aiff files sometimes.

Given the threat of malware through email attachments, it is better to send links to music files stored online in cloud-based services such as Box, Dropbox, Google Drive. These don't display lyrics, you have to add an additional file for that.

A more effective solution is offered by online cloud music catalog and pitching services. These services allow you to include comprehensive metadata and share downloadable links, all while ensuring the seamless transfer of your metadata. Our favorite catalog management solutions are SongSpace and Disco AC.

How to Add Metadata on Apple Music (iTunes) and Windows:

One of the simplest ways to attach metadata to your music files is to use a free program called Apple Music (iTunes), available on both Mac and Windows-based computers.

1) Click Command i on a Mac; right-click key+i on Windows

2) In the pop-up window, you'll see tabs across the top; select the tab to enter data into.

3) Select "Details" (default): See the following example for the fields we usually fill out.

4) Select "Artwork": Upload artwork with the title of the song.

5) Select "Lyrics": Type in or paste your lyrics.

Details Tab

Artwork Tab

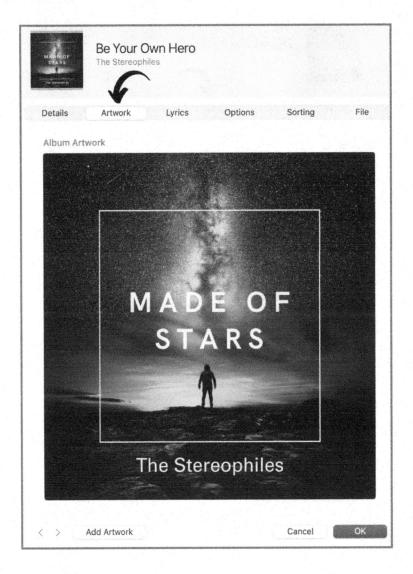

Lyrics Tab

Be Your Own Hero
The Stereophiles

Details	Artwork	Lyrics	Options	Sorting	File

Down on your knees
Hands reaching
For someone
But no one's coming
No one came to save the day
No one came to chase the trouble away

Aren't you tired of waiting?
Whoa, whoa
No answer to the prayers you're praying
Whoa, whoa

You could be your own hero
Just trust in yourself
You can rise above it all
Don't you hear your own heart calling?
It'll lift you up when you're falling
Don't need a knight in shining armor
To save you when the world gets darker
You know exactly where you need to go
You can be your own hero
Oh, oh

Face the storm
When it's coming
Now there's no more running
Find your strength when you need more
You know you've fought and you've won the war

No more desperate waiting
Whoa, whoa
Heard what your heart was saying
Whoa, whoa

You could be your own hero
Just trust in yourself

‹ › ☑ Custom Lyrics   Cancel   OK

Follow these instructions to add metadata to mp3 and wav files on a MAC.

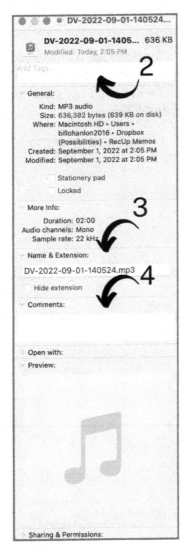

Adding Metadata from Your Desktop (MAC)

1) Select a music file and click Command "i" to open the information box.

2) Use the "Add Tags" field to input metadata.

3) In the "Name and Extension" field, you can rename the file.

4) Enter contact information in the "Comments" section.

5) By closing the pop-up, the new information will be saved.

How To Add Metadata to Your Song on DISCO.ac

Disco.ac (Disco) is a top choice for writers focusing on getting sync placements because it is widely adopted as an industry standard by sync professionals. It's a user-friendly solution for any songwriter looking to store, pitch, and effortlessly locate your own music.

Much like Apple Music, you can add a title, artist name, album title, composer/writer information, publisher names, genre, the release date, BPM, an ISRC code, and which number track the song is on the album if it is part of a collection.

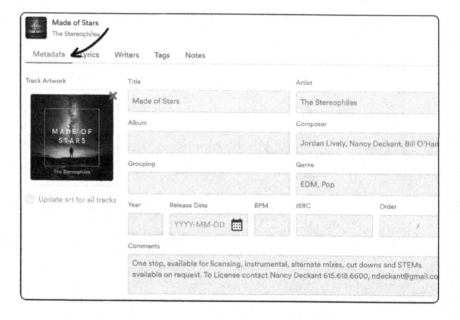

Add Lyrics to Your Song in Disco

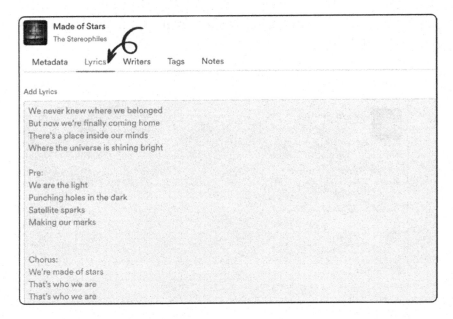

Add Tags (Metadata) to Your Song in Disco

Disco offers lists of possible meta tags that make it easy to describe and categorize your song to someone who's never heard it before. Disco also lets you create your own meta tags that remain in the system for future use.

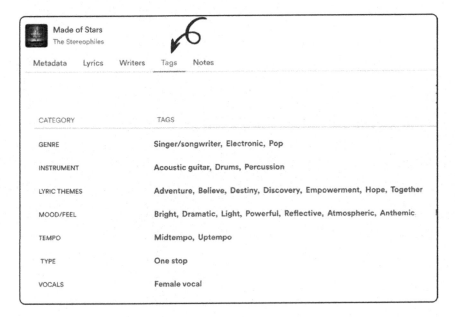

Send Trackable Links to Pitch Your Song

Once your song has been saved to Disco, you'll be offered a link to share your song.

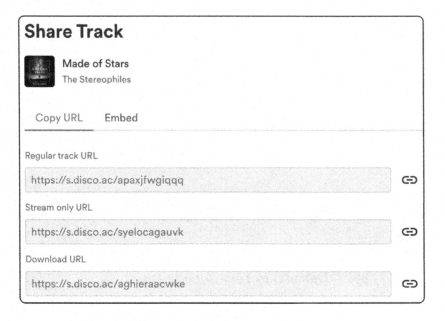

User's View of Track and Access to Lyrics:

This is what the viewer will see when they click on the link:

1. Top: Track formats (mp3, wav, aiff) can be selected and downloaded. The song or playlist can also be saved directly to the viewer's Disco account.

2. Click on the **i button** to see the lyrics.

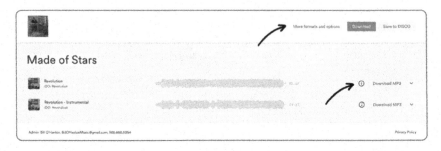

User's View of Lyrics

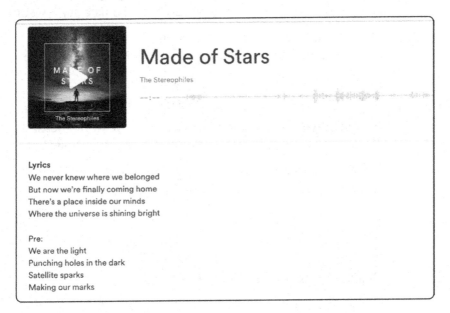

When you send a trackable link or playlist, DISCO will show how many times your song has been played and downloaded.

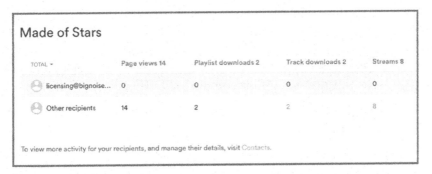

There's So Much More on Disco AC

As a songwriter serious about making relationships with music supervisors, sync agents and other industry professionals, Disco helps us look professional and makes it easy to manage our catalog. Go to our website for video tutorials.

Checklist for Sync

1) **Find your tribe.** Find fellow songwriters, producers, singers, artists writing and producing songs for sync. Then start making connections with sync agents and music supervisors.

2) **Write:** It all starts with a great song, well written, well produced, well sung. Nothing else can happen without the song.

3) **Record Masters:** Get a high-quality recording of the song.

4) **Get a signed "Work for Hire" agreement** with at least the producer and vocalist before you leave the recording studio.

5) **Get It in Writing:** Agree on percentage of ownership of composition and recording between the writers.

6) **Fill out Song Split Sheet** with an administration, pitch and one stop agreements paragraphs on it. All writers need to sign it.

7) **Register your songs** with your PRO.

8) **Get a Disco Account.** Use this link to get a discount. https://disco.ac/signup?b=20087&u=828121.

9) **Get AIFF files** of your main mix, instrumental and vocal stems and add to Disco. We love Aiff files because they usually retain all metadata when they are shared on Disco.

10) **Build your catalog** and pitch quickly to diverse briefs.

11) **Find places to pitch** your song and get live briefs. Here's two for starters: Songtradr.com and MDIIO.com.

12) **Pitch in a timely manner** and follow up quickly when invited to send in songs.

13) **Get legal help** when you're offered a licensing contract and don't sign anything that you don't like. Remember, they're not the only game in town!

14) **Beware the opportunist** wanting your publishing simply to pitch your song in the world of sync.

15) **If you are on a union project**, contact SAG-AFTRA to provide your contact information if you want to receive royalties. https://www.sagaftra.org

Chapter 8 charts and videos at https://www.nashvillecool.com/tsg

9. Industry Professionals Supporting Songwriters

Jumping into the world of music is more than just a creative endeavor; it's an adventure that relies on a team of industry professionals.

You've got your back covered by an entertainment attorney, someone to make things happen with a publisher, the organizational wizardry of publishing administrators, the hype-building prowess of song pluggers and the organizations dedicated to helping songwriters learn the craft and business of songwriting.

Everyone brings something different at various times in your journey. Let's dive in.

Organizations Dedicated to Songwriters

If you ever set foot in Nashville, you will find a community of songwriters of all stripes, venues rich in music history from Elvis to Paramore, and the ever-evolving music business.

If you're new, there are many organizations who want to help songwriters, not just for the money, but because they honestly care. Of course, be careful! There are some sour apples. But in this town, word gets around so they don't last all that long.

Here's a short list of great organizations that we have been a part of that have helped us on our way. They can help you too! Head over to our website for more. https://www.nashvillecool.com/tsg

1) **Nashville Songwriters Association International (NSAI):** Bart Herbison Executive Director. Helps songwriters learn the craft and business. https://www.nashvillesongwriters.com

2) **Global Songwriters Connection**/Sheree Spoltore, President. One-on-one career mentoring. https://globalsongwriters.com

3) **Discover Sooner**/Nancy Deckant CEO/Founder. Helps songwriters make relationships with music industry professionals. https://www.discoversooner.com

4) **Songtown**/Marty Dodson and Clay Matthews: Helps songwriters write better songs. www.songtown.com

More great programs: Green To Gold/Debbie Zavitson. Songwriting Pro/Brent Baxter. Play for Publishers/Barbara Cloyd, SongTunr/Sandy Ramos.

Entertainment Attorneys

Imagine this: You land your first gig at the local Tastee Freeze after high school, and someone drops the bombshell, "Hey, you need to get a lawyer to work in this soft-serve ice cream business!" That would never float right? But unlike most conventional jobs, acquiring a lawyer in the music business isn't a mere punchline; it's an essential step.

Music is a person-to-person business. The more successful you are as a songwriter, the more the expertise of an entertainment attorney becomes indispensable.

Without a knowledgeable guide and consultant, you risk losing both the rights to your songs and potential income. Ensuring your contracts are equitable, balanced, and address your specific requirements is essential. Here are just a few ways lawyers watch out for songwriters:

- Contract Negotiations.
- Publishing and Publishing Administration Deals.
- Royalty Disputes and Resolutions.
- Licensing Agreements: Mechanical, Sync, etc.
- Collaboration Agreements, Song Split Sheets.
- Trademarks and Copyrights.

While your brother-in-law, the divorce attorney, might know generally about legal matters and may be cheap or free, entertainment lawyers are much more familiar with the traditions, standards, and legal aspects of songwriting.

We understand that as a songwriter, budget constraints can limit your ability to hire legal help. However, consider taking a small step, such as acquiring a reusable blank mechanical license from a lawyer. Consider it an investment in a new relationship with the potential for substantial returns in the future.

Finally, we are sharing our hard-won experience as songwriters to help you protect your songs, but we are not lawyers, and nothing in this book should be taken as legal advice. Yes, we know - we keep saying the same thing!

> We have a songwriter friend who was over the moon because he had been offered his first publishing deal. He sought out an entertainment lawyer before signing the contract. It turned out that there was a clause buried in the contract that specified if the publisher changed even a word in the song or any part of the melody during the demo recording process, the publisher would become an equal co-writer on the song.
>
> The lawyer urged our friend to swiftly distance himself from both the contract and those proposing it. Our friend, a little heartbroken, did. Sometime later, he signed a much better contract with a different publisher that ended up leading to his first hit song.

Music Publishers

Music publishers are somewhat like literary agents that book authors get to represent and sell their books and maximize revenues from that book. Those literary agents not only know the business, but they have spent lots of time developing relationships with key players in the business.

Publishers play a crucial role in the music business by acquiring, promoting, and exploiting the rights to musical compositions, ensuring that songwriters receive proper compensation for the use of their work.

Publishers often buy catalogs from hit songwriters and/or sign songwriters, pitch their songs to artists, collect royalties and payments, and handle administration tasks such as registering and copyrighting songs and more.

They may also have sub-publishing deals with foreign publishers. These agreements generate extra income for songs, and the sub-publishers get a percentage of the funds collected for finding and facilitating these opportunities in foreign countries.

It can be life-changing when a publisher wants to sign you as a songwriter because of the support they offer. Here's why:

Catalog administration: They often manage all the administration paperwork and income collection from the licensing and recording of your song when it gets cut.

Schedule co-writes and maintain your writing schedule: They arrange for their writers to get with other writers, producers, or recording artists who are more likely to get cuts.

Song pluggers work to get your songs cut: They have relationships with artists and record labels that you don't have and can more readily get your song to artists.

Financial support via monthly draw and a demo budget: They may pay you each month and deduct that amount from the actual income your songs make now or in the future. Many times publishers don't get paid back if your songs don't reach the radio, but you never owe this money back. Publishers take the risk on you.

Most of the time these deals are reserved for writers who already have hits, or the publisher is sure they can place a song by a writer.

Publishing Administrators

The more intentional you are about the creative side of songwriting, the more you need a seasoned publishing professional managing the business side for you.

If your songs are being cut by artists and generating income, or one of your songs is about to have significant income with a major label artist, you can enter into a publishing administrative agreement with just about any publisher.

Many publishers have the infrastructure in place to handle the paperwork and collect the money your song is owed. Their fee is usually around 15% of the "publishing income" collected from the song, although it could be higher or lower. They don't take fees from the writer's share.

You can handle many of the administrative activities listed below on your own. But a great publishing administrator "admin" can usually do the job better and faster!

- Register your songs with your PRO.
- Register commercially released songs with The MLC and SoundExchange (if you're an artist).
- Collect U.S. and international royalties.
- Issue mechanical licenses and sync licenses for videos and negotiate with artists.
- Review sync licenses and negotiate with music supervisors.
- Apply for composition copyrights and phonograms with the Library of Congress.
- Sometimes admins actively look for song placements too.

Music Distributors as Publishing Administrators

SongTrust and music distributors like CDBaby, TuneCore offer publishing administration to self-administered songwriters.

These "retail" products collect both mechanical and performance royalties from your PRO, The MLC, SoundExchange, Foreign MROs and charge an industry standard of about 15% on the proceeds they collect. They are particularly valuable when gathering international mechanical royalties.

The biggest drawback to these publishing administrators isn't their fee. Our concern is that you may lose sync placements when music supervisors see that you have a publishing administrator, like CDBaby or TuneCore, who will not be available to sign licensing agreements when they want to license your song for their movie.

If you don't care about getting your music into TV and movies, then there's no problem. But if you do want sync placements, music supervisors run the other way seeing that you have a publishing administrator like this because they do not respond quickly. Nancy reached out to SongTrust for a work-around. Six weeks later she received the following answer:

"A good work-around for this would be to register the works (songs) that you are pitching to sync, directly with your PRO so that the clearance stage is a lot smoother. You can, afterwards, register your work with SongTrust so that you can collect your global royalties." – The SongTrust Team.

Sounds good, kinda. But who knows what songs you'll want to try to get into TV/film? Ugh, such a challenge! You decide what's best for you.

Song Pluggers

If you're exclusively a songwriter without plans to record your own music, connecting with a song plugger is crucial to have your songs recorded, released, and performed.

Song pluggers specialize in placing songs with artists and securing sync placements. They leverage extensive industry relationships to connect with artists through record labels, and producers.

Independent song pluggers usually charge a fee and/or ask for a percentage of the songwriter's publishing. You can vet song pluggers by asking experienced songwriter friends and industry professionals on who to avoid. There are people who take advantage of desperate songwriters. Remember, if you feel urgent, it's not the right time to for you get a song plugger! Instead, do what professional songwriters do.

1) Educate yourself on what artists record songs like you write.

2) Listen to every song the artist has ever recorded so you're not pitching a topic they already sang about.

3) Learn everything you can learn about the artist from news sources on Google. If they just got married, they are not going to want to sing your break-up song!

4) Write, write, and write songs that are down that artist's lane.

5) Buy an hour of mentoring from an independent publisher (usually about $100) and play your work-tapes for them. If they fall off their chair and want to pitch your song, you can demo that song; while having avoided spending money on songs that don't make the cut. If the publisher sends you back to work on your songs, you're not ready for a song plugger yet. Write more songs. Go to organizations like Discover Sooner for mentoring programs.

Record Labels

Record labels sign, develop, and promote musical acts for recording, release, and performances. They engage in merchandise sales, tours, sync licensing, writing retreats, marketing, social media management, and publicity. A&R personnel are tasked with discovering exceptional songs for artists. Getting signed by a record label is challenging due to the significant investment of money, time, and effort in each artist.

Artist Managers

Artist managers play a vital role in shaping musicians' careers, serving as strategic partners and advocates in the dynamic music industry. They influence every aspect of an artist's life, from negotiating contracts to building fan base to diversifying revenue.

Booking Agents

Booking agents secure live performance opportunities for artists, acting as intermediaries between artists and event organizers. They negotiate contracts and coordinate logistics to ensure successful concerts and tours.

Go to our website for a list of music industry professionals from Chapter 9. https://www.nashvillecool.com/tsg

10. Your Publisher Playbook

The dream of every aspiring professional songwriter is to have their songs recorded and released into the world and get paid for it! To get paid, a Mechanical License needs to be issued.

Because we all need instructions that won't make us question our life choices, below is a step-by-step guide that will help you get the job done.

When Is a Mechanical License Needed?

Outside Artist: Whenever someone you don't know wants to release a song you wrote, they need to get a mechanical license from you.

Co-writer Artist: If any co-writer wants to release a song you wrote, they need a Mechanical License from you.

When Is a Mechanical License Not Needed?

You As the Artist and Solo Writer: If you are an artist and the solo writer of the song, a Mechanical License is *not required.* **However,** we suggest your publishing company license the song to you - the artist. Why? Because in the future, you may want to sell your catalog, and this is a paper trail of your released songs. The more songs in your catalog, the more your catalog is worth.

Public Domain Songs: If you want to record an old song with an expired copyright, you don't need a mechanical license.

Step by Step Guide for Issuing Mechanical Licenses and Releasing a Song through a Music Distributor

This guide covers all of the publishing steps, the steps to release the recording, and the remaining steps self-administered songwriters should take if they have not already done so, to increase their income. Some steps may not apply to your situation:

1) If the song was co-written and it's the first use of the song, check with your co-writers and their publishers to be sure everyone's on board with licensing the song.

2) All co-writers should issue their own mechanical license to the artist because no one wants to be responsible for collecting another person's royalties.

3) Work with the artist/label/team to determine what configuration of product will be released (downloads, CD vinyl, etc.) and the number of reproductions.

   a) For indie artist releases, it's strongly advised to collect an advance on units sold. You'll want to be pre-paid for at least 1,000 units.

   b) For major label artists, quarterly payments are made because they have the accounting systems and personnel to manage payments. They will most likely issue the license.

4) Determine the latest statutory royalty rate for the type of product. In 2024, the royalty is $12.4 cents per CD, vinyl or digital download, etc.

5) Get the project information from the Artist: Title, Record #, Artist Label Name, Address, Recording Duration, ISRC, UPC, Release Date.

6) Verify your songwriter info and splits: PRO Writer IPI/CAE and publisher IPI/CAE and the song's ISWC code. Use the song split sheet if you have one.

7) Issue the Mechanical License to the artist for the agreed upon number of reproductions. See Chapter 3 for an agreement and details.

8) Check with your PRO to see if the song has been listed already. If listed, retrieve the info for your mechanical license.

If it's not listed, register the song with your PRO (BMI, ASCAP).

9) Check The MLC to see if the song has been listed already. If it's listed, claim the song. If not, register your portion of the song.

10) Copyright your composition © through the Library of Congress. Split the cost with co-writers.

11) Sheet Music: If you have sheet music, sign up for an account on MusicNotes.com.

12) Lyrics: Register your song with LyricFind.com, also accessible via Distrokid.

13) If you are recording owner (artist, label, sync team):

   a) Use one of the Distribution services like CDBaby, DistroKid, TuneCore etc. to digitally distribute your song. Make sure to get the release date, track#, UPC and ISRC for the mechanical license.

   b) Check any boxes that give permission for your song to be played on Twitter, Facebook, Instagram, TikTok, YouTube, etc. Royalties will be processed through your PRO.

   c) If you share ownership of the recording, make sure you use "splits" to forward income generated by the recording in the agreed upon percentages to the producer, musicians, non-featured vocalists, co-writers, investors, etc.

   d) Register your percentage of the song with SoundExchange.com.

   e) Copyright your phonogram ℗ through the Library of Congress.

14) Join the NMPA.org and Music Reports Inc. if you haven't already, to be eligible to make income through opt-in agreements. See Chapter 7 for details.

15) Issuing Sync Licenses for YouTube: If someone wants to feature a song you wrote in their YouTube video, they'll need to secure a sync license agreement from the song's co-writers.

   a) The only way to secure a sync license is by directly reaching out to the publisher(s) of the songwriters.

Publishers have the authority to establish any price, take as much time as needed, or decline the license entirely.

b) As the licensor, you will need to decide how much to charge the recording owner. It can be an amount upfront and/or a percentage of the ad revenue usually 15-20% split between co-writers.

c) Chapter 11 has a sample Sync License for YouTube. It's pretty straightforward. Check it out!

Chapter 10 charts and videos at https://www.nashvillecool.com/tsg

11. Essential Agreements

There's the creative side of songwriting and there's the business side. Many creative individuals struggle with the details of crossing every 't' and dotting every 'i'. But to avoid losing income and future legal issues, it's crucial for us to become good at managing the business. We need to get agreements in writing. As Richard Marx infamously said, "It doesn't mean anything until they sign it on the dotted line."

Beware of one-sided contracts. Remember, it's only a piece of paper! You can ask for changes. Bill has signed many literary publishing contracts and was surprised the first time he got one back from his legal representative how many changes were asked for. About half of the contract had sections and phrases crossed out and there were new sections and wording added. The contract and negotiations went back and forth until all parties were satisfied and then it was signed.

So, let's put our publisher pants on and paper-up people! The following is a set of basic agreements.

Consult with a legal professional to ensure compliance with local laws and to address the specifics of your situation:

1) Song Split Sheet.

2) Sync Administration Agreement (for use between songwriters).

3) Song & Recording Ownership Split Agreement.

4) Work For Hire Agreement.

5) Sync License for use of composition on YouTube.

6) Publishing Deal (too complex to cover but some key considerations discussed).

7) Mechanical License (see Chapter 3).

Song Split Sheets for Co-writers

Self-administered songwriters regularly miss opportunities to get their songs recorded or placed in TV shows, movies, commercials/ads, and video games because they couldn't contact their co-writers years after the song was written, or they didn't have the co-writer's PRO information.

When we co-write with others, what we all need is a song split sheet that reflects who wrote the song, the percentage of ownership, each writers' PRO information and contact information.

SAMPLE: SONG SPLIT SHEET

Song Title: The Journey

Percentage (%) Of Agreed & Assigned Splits
Songwriters: Nancy Deckant, 33.34% Bill O'Hanlon, 33.33% Leslie Bowe, 33.33%
Publishers: Nashville Cool Music 33.34%, O'Hanlon and O'Hanlon Music, 33.33% LEB Music, 33.33%

Owner's PRO and Contact Information
Legal Name, - Affiliation - IPI/CAE - Contact

Writer Legal Name: Bill O'Hanlon – BMI - 01006139110
Publisher: O Hanlon and O Hanlon Music - BMI - 00896183682
Phone: (505) ###-#### Email: BillOHanlonMusic@gmail.com

Writer Legal Name: Nancy Deckant - BMI - 511978444
Publisher: Nashville Cool Music - BMI - 367539716
Phone: (615) ###-#### Email: Nancy@NashvilleCool.com

Writer Legal Name: Leslie Earl Bowe - BMI - 00241490684
Publisher: LEB Music - BMI - 00182581262
Phone: (615) ###-#### Email: lesliebowemusic@gmail.com

Agreed to by: (Sign and Date)

[Your Full Name]
[Your Signature]/Date

[Your Full Name]
[Your Signature]/Date

Recording Ownership Agreement

A Recording Master Ownership Agreement outlines the ownership and rights related to a recording. This agreement is particularly relevant in the music industry where artists, producers, and record labels collaborate to create and distribute recordings.

SAMPLE: COMPOSITION & RECORDING SPLIT AGREEMENT

Song Title: [Enter song title here]

Date Recorded: [dd/mm/yyyy]

The undersigned songwriters and recording owners hereby affirm and acknowledge that exclusive contributions to the song titled above were made solely by us on the specified date.

We mutually agree on the distribution of ownership percentages as outlined below. It is explicitly understood that any recordings made outside the mentioned date are not subject to joint ownership.

Percentage (%) Of Agreed & Assigned Splits

Songwriter percentage ownership%
X% Cowriter's Name, PRO, IPI/CAE
X% Cowriter's Name, PRO, IPI/CAE
X% Cowriter's Name, PRO, IPI/CAE

Publisher % - X%
X% Publishing Co. Name, PRO, IPI/CAE
X% Publishing Co. Name, PRO, IPI/CAE
X% Publishing Co. Name, PRO, IPI/CAE

Copyright ownership of Recording Master %
X% Cowriter's Name
X% Cowriter's Name
X% Cowriter's Name

Acknowledged and Agreed:

[Your Full Name]
[Your Signature]/Date

[Your Full Name]
[Your Signature]/Date

Sync Administration Agreements Between Songwriters

When a music supervisor wants to use your song in a movie, TV, game, or any audio-visual medium, licensing can move very quickly.

The licensing agent typically requires a quick decision, often within hours. Therefore, having a pre-existing agreement with your co-writers and master co-owners is critical.

Many songwriters add this administration agreement to their song split sheet agreement so that the information is all in one place.

SAMPLE: ADMINISTRATION AGREEMENT FOR SYNC PLACEMENTS AND LICENSING

[names of songwriters] all have administration rights to pitch and agree to contracts and placements for our co-written song **"[song title/or list of song titles]**."

We collectively hold shares in the creation, publishing, and master recording of this song. Each writer possesses the authority to present this song for non-exclusive licensing opportunities, is authorized to sign licenses on behalf of their fellow creators, and is capable of granting written approval on behalf of the entire group.

[Your Full Name]
[Your Signature]/Date

[Your Full Name]
[Your Signature]/Date

[Your Full Name]
[Your Signature]/Date

"One Stop" Agreement

In sync, we often use "One Stop" agreements that allow any one of us to sign off on any licensing paperwork on behalf of each other. That doesn't mean we're the DECIDER. We fully communicate with each other throughout the negotiations.

SAMPLE: ONE STOP AGREEMENT FOR NON-EXCLUSIVE SYNC PLACEMENTS AND LICENSING

[names of songwriters] all have administration rights to pitch and agree to contracts and placements for our co-written song **"[song title/or list of song titles]."**

We own 100% of the writing, publishing and recording shares of this song.

We have provided complete authorization to **[full names of cowriters]**, granting each individual the independent authority to endorse and finalize any NON-EXCLUSIVE synchronization of the composition and/or master use licensing for the master recording agreements on behalf of all participating songwriters, publishers, and recording owners.

Each co-writer is fully capable of promptly and unequivocally granting 100% clearance and presenting the recording as a "ONE STOP" option on a non-exclusive basis.

[Your Full Name]
[Your Signature]/Date

[Your Full Name]
[Your Signature]/Date

[Your Full Name]
[Your Signature]/Date

Work For Hire Agreement

When you hire individuals to work on a recording, such as a producer, session players, vocalists, mix and mastering engineers, it's important to get a Work For Hire Agreement signed upfront.

SAMPLE: VOCALIST/PRODUCER/PLAYER WORK FOR HIRE AGREEMENT

This agreement is entered into on_____ day of _____, _____, for good and valuable consideration, the receipt and adequacy of which are here acknowledged between (**name of performer**) hereinafter referred to as the "Performer", acting as a (**vocalist/musician/producer**) and (**recipient name**) hereinafter referred to as the "Recipient" who agree as follows:

For the song titled: (**Title of Song**)
And Performer's name to be credited as: (**performer's stage name**)

1) Performer acknowledges receipt of full and complete compensation of (**amount**) for his or her creative services and hereby waives and releases all rights and claims to any copyright, royalty, and other remuneration relating to the use, sale, assignment, license and/or other exploitation of the work(s).

2) Performer agrees that their performance is "Work For Hire" as defined in Section 101 of the United States Copyright Act and grants to Recipient, its successors and assigns, absolutely and forever, all rights of every kind and nature of Performer's services and performances.

The Performer hereby grants the Recipient the right to use their name, image, likeness, and biographical information in any tangible or intangible reproductions of the song and in all promotional materials associated with the song. Select one:

YES_____ NO_____

3) Parties agree to indemnify each other, along with successors, licensees, and assignees, from all claims, liabilities, damages, costs, or expenses arising from any breach of representations, warranties, or agreements made under this agreement.

4) This Agreement shall be governed by and construed in accordance with the laws of the (**State**). Any action under this Agreement shall be brought in (**County**), whose courts shall have exclusive jurisdiction over any dispute arising here from.

5) This Agreement constitutes the entire understanding between the parties and supersedes all prior negotiations and understandings.

6) This Agreement may be executed in separate counterparts, each of which shall be deemed as original, but all of which taken together shall constitute one and the same instrument.

AGREED AND ACCEPTED

Performer: [Performer's Name]
Signature/Date
Recipient: [Recipient's Name or Company Name]
Signature/Date

YouTube Sync Agreement

Here is a sync agreement granting the recording owner permission to use your composition.

SAMPLE: YOUTUBE SYNC AGREEMENT

This Sync Agreement ("Agreement") is entered into on [Date], by and between:

[Your Name or Company Name]
[Your Address]
[City, State, Zip Code]
[Email Address]
[Phone Number]
("Licensee") and

[Composer's Name or Company Name]
[Composer's Address]
[Composer's Email Address]
[Composer's Phone Number]
("Licensor")

(collectively referred to as the "Parties").

BACKGROUND:

Licensee owns the rights to the composition described as follows:
- Title: [Title of the Composition]
- Composer: [Name of the Composer]
- Creation Date: [Date of Composition]

Licensor desires to use the composition in a video to be uploaded to YouTube.

AGREEMENT TERMS:

1) **Grant of License:** Licensee hereby grants Licensor a world-wide non-exclusive license to use the composition in the YouTube video titled "[Title of the YouTube Video]." This license includes the right to synchronize the composition with visual content in the video.

2) **Territory:** This license is granted for worldwide use.

3) **Duration:** The license is granted for a period of [Number] years, starting from the date of execution of this Agreement.

4) **Usage Restrictions:** Licensor agrees not to use the composition for any purpose other than as expressly stated in this Agreement. The license is non-transferable, and Licensor may not sublicense the rights granted herein.

5) **Consideration:** In consideration for the rights granted, Licensor agrees to pay Licensee the sum of [Amount] as compensation for the use of the composition. Payment shall be made within [Number] days of the execution of this Agreement.

6) **Credit and Promotion:** Licensor agrees to credit the composition in the video description on YouTube as follows: "Composition: [Title] by [Composer], used with permission."

7) **Notices:** All notices or communications required or permitted by this Agreement shall be in writing and sent to the addresses listed at the beginning of this Agreement or to such other address as either Party may designate by notice to the other.

8) **Governing Law:** This Agreement shall be governed by and construed in accordance with the laws of the [State/Country] whose courts shall have exclusive jurisdiction over any dispute arising here from.

9) **Indemnification:** Parties agree to indemnify each other, along with successors, licensees, and assignees, from all claims, liabilities, damages, costs, or expenses arising from any breach of representations, warranties, or agreements made under this agreement.

10) **Entire Agreement:** This Agreement constitutes the entire understanding between the parties and supersedes all prior negotiations and understandings.

11) **Counterparts:** This Agreement may be executed in separate counterparts, each of which shall be deemed as original, but all of which taken together shall constitute one and the same instrument.

IN WITNESS WHEREOF, the Parties hereto have executed this Sync Agreement as of the date first above written.

Licensee: [Your Name or Company Name]
Signature/Date

Licensor: [Composer's Name or Company Name]
Signature/Date

Major Points of Publishing Deals

As a songwriter you own both your writer's share and your publishing share of the song, unless you assigned all or part of your publishing to a publisher.

If you are offered a publishing deal, you will receive a very long and detailed contract. Get an attorney specializing in entertainment law to represent you BEFORE you sign anything!

Every publishing deal has different terms, so we are not providing a sample of a contract.

But be aware that songs written before your publishing deal are typically listed on an addendum called a Schedule A. If those songs are already earning income, you can negotiate different compensation for Schedule A songs, than the songs written under the pub deal.

The downside of having a publisher is that you can be locked into an agreement that doesn't serve you. Maybe you're not the publisher's highest priority, the publisher doesn't actively pitch your songs or get you any co-writes or you're just not on the same page. There are pitfalls with any relationship. Take it slow before signing!

Sample Agreements

Go to our website to download all of the agreements in this book and from Chapter 11.

https://www.nashvillecool.com/tsg

12. Five Easy Fixes for Common Problems

We trust you have probably already started navigating the songwriting business and are taking the steps needed to protect your songs and collect every last royalty due to you!

Here's a list of "Dos" that will empower your career in music.

1) **Stay Out of the Black Box!** Make sure your IPI/CAE and song's ISWC AND ISRC codes are correct on all licenses.

2) **Register Your Live Play Set List with your PRO:** It's hard to find time to do this. Check out your PRO's app. It may make registering your set lists easier.

3) **When You Pitch Songs, Include Your Contact Info and Writer/Publisher PRO In MP3 And Links:** Self-administered songwriters regularly lose opportunities because their contact info isn't in the mp3 or link sent to a music industry professional. Double check!

4) **Use Song Split Sheets to Give Your Co-Writers "One Stop" Permissions:** If we can all say "Yes" to placement opportunities, we'll all make more money with our music.

5) **Educate And Empower Your Heirs:** Once you write a song, it is your intellectual property. Just like other pieces of property you own, like your house and car. Make sure to include your music in your estate planning and will.

Leave clear instructions for your heirs on how you want your music to be managed. Maybe leave them a copy of this book so they can educate themselves. And include a list of reputable publishing administrators they can work with that you can find on our website.

Let's not forget your co-writers; they'll need a guardian angel with the ability to approve licenses when you've graduated to the great gig in the sky!

Closing Thoughts and an Invitation

As we wrap up this final chapter, we want to convey our excitement over the prospect of you immersing yourself in these pages and feeling more confident about managing your publishing.

Forgive us our typos and grant us grace for any mistakes. Music publishing is vast and we're trying to hit the highlights here! We're counting on you to provide feedback for improvements that we'll be sure to post updates on our website.

Please let us know your thoughts and any other topic related to songwriters and the music business you'd like to learn about.

Please leave us a testimonial wherever you bought the book. It will make a big difference to us!

Remember that links to websites and tutorials on the internet **can and do expire**. Go to our website for videos, charts and links from this book and to download all of the agreements in this book.

Keep the creative spirit alive. And don't forget, music thrives on shared joy and creativity. Make sure you have lots of fun with those who write it, play it, live it, and love it!

Contact Us
https://www.nashvillecool.com/tsg

Glossary of Terms

Artist/Writer: Also known as a singer/songwriter, is a songwriter who writes and records songs.

BMI Live/ASCAP On Stage/SESAC Live Performance Notification Log: An online services application that allows performing songwriters to submit their live performance information and receive royalty payments from their PROs.

Composition: Works that have a medley consisting of words and music (i.e. a song), or any dramatic material and bridging passages, whether in form of instrumental and/or vocal music, prose or otherwise, irrespective of length.

Compulsory License: The non-exclusive control over who gets to record and release the song after the first official audio-only recording of the work. Agencies like HFA & Songfile can issue mechanical licenses of cover songs after the first use of the song has been granted. Or you can obtain compulsory licenses directly from the publisher of the song.

Copyright: The exclusive legal right, given to an originator or an assignee to print, publish, perform, film, or record literary, artistic, or musical material, and to authorize others to do the same.

DSPs (Digital Streaming Providers): Online platforms such as Spotify, Apple, Amazon, Deezer, etc. obtain rights to stream or enable the download of music, supported by revenue from paid subscribers and advertisements.

EasySong.com: A simple way to obtain mechanical licenses for less than 2,500 CDs and vinyl plus digital downloads.

First Use or "the Right of First Release": The right to determine the when, where and who of the song's first public release which is held by the publisher(s) of the songwriters who wrote the song.

Harry Fox Agency (HFA): Mechanical Rights Organization that issues mechanical licenses for more than 2,500 physical units, downloads, ringtones or 10,000 units.

Interactive Streaming: When a user chooses exactly what they want to listen to on subscription-based services like Spotify and Apple Music.

IPI/CAE number: A number your PRO assigns to you as a writer that is used to track and connect your songs, so you get payments. You can also have a separate IPI/CAE number for the publisher of your song.

ISRC (International Standard Recording Code) number: This is a number (and usually has a bar code with it) that is issued to songs that are released on audio or video.

Master or Master Recording: See Recording

Mechanical Licensing Collective (MLC): A nonprofit organization designated by the U.S. Copyright Office to collect digital mechanical royalties in the United States pursuant to the Music Modernization Act of 2018.

Mechanical Royalties: Royalties earned through the reproduction of copyrighted works in digital and physical formats.

Metadata: The set of information corresponding to a song file, such as artist name, producer, writer, song title, release date and more, used to identify, sort and deliver your audio content. The more comprehensive the metadata, the easier the collection and distribution of royalties to rights holders.

Music Distributors: Online music distribution services that make recorded music available to the public via the internet. Examples: DistroKid, TuneCore and CDBaby, etc.

Non-Interactive Streaming: When a user cannot choose what songs are played next. Examples: Online radio, Satellite: Sirius XM, & Pandora (free version).

Performing Rights Organization (PRO): A PRO is an agency that ensures songwriters and publishers are paid for the use of their songs (musical compositions) by collecting royalties on behalf of the rights owner.

Publisher Share: In a composition, the "Publisher Share" is the business side of the song that manages royalties and licensing.

Publishing Royalties: Royalties earned through the exploitation of a song's musical composition copyright.

Recording (aka Sound Recording, Master, Master Recording): Works that result from the fixation of a series of musical, spoken, or other sounds but not including sounds accompanying a motion picture or other audiovisual work (i.e. digital and physical formats). The Recording is copyright protected by the ℗ copyright.

Rights Holder: A rights holder for songs is an individual or entity that owns and controls the legal rights associated with a particular song which can include songwriters, composers, music publishers, recording artists (if they also wrote the song), and record labels (if they own the master recording).

Royalty: Payments to rights holders (songwriters, publishers, composers, recording artists, and their representatives) in exchange for the licensed use of their music.

Self-Released Artist: A songwriter who sings the song and owns the recording and doesn't have a record label.

Songfile.com: A simple way to obtain mechanical licenses for a limited number CDs and vinyl plus digital downloads made and distributed in the U.S., as well as ringtones, permanent downloads ("PDDs") of singles, and certain interactive streams. Used for up to 2,500 physical units, downloads, ringtones or 10,000 units for interactive streaming.

Song Split Sheet: A written agreement that identifies each contributor to a song and establishes ownership percentages amongst them. The agreed percentages determine how much each contributor will receive from the royalties generated by their music.

Songtrust: A global publishing administrator that registers songs on behalf of their members with more than 60 pay sources around the world - including Performance Rights Organizations (PROs), mechanical collection societies, and digital streaming providers.

SoundExchange: Collects and distributes digital performance royalties for non-interactive streaming on internet radio, Pandora, cable and satellite radio.

Streaming: A service that focuses primarily on music, and sometimes other forms of digital audio content. Examples: Spotify, Apple Music & Amazon Music.

Sync Fee/Sync Licensing Fee: A one-time payment for the use of copyrighted music in audiovisual productions such as DVDs, television shows, films, advertisements, and video games.

Work For Hire (WFH): Agreements that are common in film, TV, and advertising, in which production companies often hire composers to create music specifically for their projects. Instead of receiving an initial fee and subsequent royalties, a work-for-hire creator receives only a one- time up-front fee for their work.

Works Registration: It provides all of the data necessary by a writer/publisher of a song to a PRO or Mechanical Rights Society to track the royalties generated by the song.

Writer Share: "Writer Share" is the creative part of the song, the lyrics and melody.

About The Authors

Bill O'Hanlon

For over five decades, Bill O'Hanlon has immersed himself in playing guitar and piano and writing songs. In recent years, he focused even more deliberately on songwriting, accumulating an ever-growing 1,600+ catalog of recorded songs.

Bill's music has secured 100+ cuts to date with artists. He works with sync co-writing/production teams, such as IDO and DOLL and has achieved hundreds of songs signed to sync agencies and 14+ sync placements including Busch Family Brewed (MTV), Call Me Kat (Fox), Love in Tahiti (Indie).

In 2022 Bill was selected as Songtown's "Songwriter of the Year". His great hooks, fresh song ideas and generosity have earned him a spot among his note-worthy co-writers including Tom Douglas, Gary Burr, Marty Dodson, Clay Mills, Phil Barton, Mark Irwin, Jason Duke, Georgia Middleman, Bobby Tomberlin, Lee Thomas Miller, Keesy Timmer, Tim James, Marti Jane Dodson, and many others.

Formerly a psychotherapist and speaker, Bill traveled the world for 30+ years before putting his work online. His significant contributions include the acclaimed book "Do One Thing Different" which landed Bill and the book on Oprah. Bill has written 41 books with 4 on songwriting (including this one).

"Song Building: Mastering Lyric Writing"
https://www.amazon.com/Song-Building-Mastering-SongTown-Songwriting-ebook/dp/B07WJWQB78/

"Mastering Melody Writing" co-written with Marty Dodson & Clay Mills
https://www.amazon.com/Mastering-Melody-Writing-Songwriters-Repetition/dp/1098364333/

"The Songwriter's Guide to Mastering Co-Writing"
https://www.amazon.com/Songwriters-Guide-Mastering-Co-Writing-Techniques-ebook/dp/B07N6N4L23/

Free video on how to add "furniture" to your song.
https://billohanlon.ck.page/songwriting

Bill divides his time between homes in Santa Fe, New Mexico, Nashville and Bonaire in the Caribbean.

Find Bill O'Hanlon
Website: www.BillOHanlonMusic.com
FB https://www.facebook.com/bill.ohanlon
IG: @ohanlonbill
YouTube: @PossiBill

Nancy Deckant

Passion and dedication are woven into everything Nancy Deckant has done throughout her 20-year career in the music industry. She is a music publisher and songwriter with two decades of invaluable music industry experience.

Her songwriting achievements include top 40 Billboard hits like "Princess" by Dallas Remington and "Hangin' Moons" by Cody Clayton Eagle, amassing millions of streams, Trinity Wiseman's "Little Too Late" and "Ghosting", "Roots" by Jason Campbell and many more. Her song "We Are The Stars", co-written with Anelda Spence, won the Independent International Songwriters Competition, Pop Category.

Nancy loves bringing people together and in 2020, she launched Discover Sooner.com a platform designed to facilitate connections between career-focused songwriters and publishers. Since its inception, the company has successfully introduced over a thousand songwriters to music industry professionals.

In her adopted hometown of Pittsburgh PA, Nancy was the Workshop Co-coordinator for the Pittsburgh Chapter of Nashville Songwriters Association International (NSAI). She moved to Nashville in 2013, wrote songs and gained invaluable publishing experience as an independent song plugger for hit songwriters.

Nancy holds an MBA from Carnegie Mellon University's Tepper School of Business, specializing in Entrepreneurship and a chemistry degree from the University of South Florida.

Prior to music, she gained a decade of experience as a process engineer for a medical device company and eight years in product marketing, primarily working with startup ventures.

Nancy's hobbies include being in the Crazy Cookie Crew (band) and doing art with friends.

Find Nancy Deckant
Email: nancy@nashvillecool.com
Nashville Cool! https://www.nashvillecool.com/
Discover Sooner https://www.discoversooner.com/
Nancy's art https://nancydeckant.com/
Spotify: Crazy Cookie Crew
@discoversooner
@nancydeckant
@crazycookiecrewmusic (Instagram); @crazycookiecrew (YouTube)

Leslie Bowe

Leslie Bowe is a passionate singer, songwriter, who is steadfastly pursuing his dreams in the vibrant music scene of Nashville.

He's a part of the Music Row scene in Nashville playing at The Bluebird Café, BNA Arrivals to Music City, Commodore Grille, Bobby's Idle Hour & The Musicians Corner in Nashville's Centennial Park concert series.

Originally from Pittsburgh, Pennsylvania, Leslie made the bold move to Music City in 2017 to embark on a journey towards a professional songwriting career.

Leslie's dedication to songwriting reflects not only in his individual pursuit but also in the collaborative spirit he brings to the vibrant community of musicians in Nashville.

Leslie has independently released five CDs: "Wings of your Dreams", "Through My Eyes", "Gypsy", "Color of Sound" and most recently the EP, "Something Right". He has opened or shared the stage with such artists as Ben Harper and Patty Griffin. His songs can be found on all available streaming platforms.

As a songwriter, Leslie received Nashville Songwriters Association International's (NSAI) prestigious 2020 evaluator Song of the Year Award for his song, "Been".

Leslie has also recently had his songs recorded and released by the Darrin Morris Band for the Top 20 hit, "I Can Drink in This Bar" which peaked at #11 on the American Country Music Chart (ACM) and #16 on the Texas Country Music Chart (TCM), Artist Kevin Herchen for the song, "Betcha", No Bounds Band for the song, "Blind Love" and more coming!

Leslie's first book is "**An Easy-to-Follow Guide to Understanding Music Song Royalties**" https://store.bookbaby.com/book/an-easy-to-follow-guide-to-understanding-music-song-royalties

Join his Facebook community Artist/Songwriter for discussion and networking.

Find Leslie Bowe
Website: www.lesliebowe.com
Email: leslieboweinfo@gmail.com
Spotify: https://open.spotify.com/artist/22JIva62FHii1bQ5n7jtur
www.itunes.apple.com/us/artist/leslie-bowe/id18947569
Instagram: www.instagram.com/leslieb0we